P9-CFX-275

Robert's Rules in Plain English

Second Edition

Robert's Rules in Plain English

Second Edition

Doris P. Zimmerman
Professional Registered Parliamentarian, Ret.

Medical Library
North Memorial Health Care
3300 Oakdale Avenue North
Robbinsdale, MN 55422

Collins
An Imprint of HarperCollins*Publishers*

JF515
Z72r
2nd ed.

ROBERT'S RULES IN PLAIN ENGLISH, SECOND EDITION. Copyright ©2005 by Doris P. Zimmerman. All rights reserved. Printed in the United States of America. No part of this book may be used or reproduced in any manner whatsoever without written permission except in the case of brief quotations embodied in critical articles and reviews. For information, address HarperCollins Publishers, 10 East 53rd Street, New York, NY 10022.

HarperCollins books may be purchased for educational, business, or sales promotional use. For information please write: Special Markets Department, HarperCollins Publishers, 10 East 53rd Street, New York, NY 10022.

Designed by Nancy Singer Olaguera

Library of Congress Cataloging-in-Publication Data has been applied for.

ISBN-10 0-06-078779-1
ISBN-13 978-0-06-078779-0

---

06 07 08 09 ISPN/OPM 10 9 8 7 6 5 4

16829

This book is dedicated to everyone who has served as a member or leader of a group, and who has, at one time or another, felt ignorant, ineffectual, helpless, frustrated, repressed, or just plain bored.

3-21-07

CONTENTS

ACKNOWLEDGMENTS

I am indebted to General Henry M. Robert for his inspiration to compile the first *Robert's Rules*. I am especially grateful to my first teacher of parliamentary procedure, the late Margaret W. Wheelock, who made it come alive for me.

I also want to thank my husband for his support and patience during my career as a parliamentarian and his belief in this book. As a convention parliamentarian, I often had to travel, leaving him to fend for himself and two dogs.

With failing vision, this second edition would have been impossible without the patient and cheerful help of Edie Windsor and Jean Hewitt, who dealt with my cranky laptop.

Last, I thank my editor, Greg Chaput, whose thoughtful suggestions and guidance were of immeasurable help. I will always be grateful to Rob Kaplan, editor of the first edition, who introduced me to publishing.

INTRODUCTION

General Robert became interested in parliamentary procedure the same way that most of us do. He was asked to preside at a meeting and he didn't know how. "My embarrassment was supreme. I plunged in, trusting to Providence that the Assembly would behave itself."

Interest in parliamentary procedure usually begins when people have a need for the knowledge. Perhaps you are elected chairman of the board or president of an organization. You now need the tools to do a good job if you want to have a productive term that strengthens the group. You must know how to plan a meeting and how to run one in an efficient and democratic manner. How does a presiding officer stay in control of the floor? What is his role in keeping the group focused on the motion at hand?

Perhaps you have been elected as secretary or treasurer of a group. Are you sure of your duties and the proper form for minutes or a treasurer's report?

Or, it may be that you are a member of a committee, board, or group that has important issues to decide. Have you ever sat through a meeting and were unhappy with the outcome? You probably remained silent because you did not know the proper way to correct a situation. Do you know what motions may be made to handle or change important questions on the floor?

These are the kinds of problems that will be addressed in this book. The proper use of parliamentary procedure will facilitate your meetings and make your organization more efficient, effective, and cohesive. It is the distilled knowledge of twenty years experience as a Professional Registered Parliamentarian. The book is written for the busy layman who does not have time to wade through the 643 pages of *Robert's Rules of Order Newly Revised. Only the essential rules and motions needed to prevent meetings from going astray are presented.* Those necessary parliamentary rules will be covered in an abbreviated form with a minimum of parliamentary jargon. Since some parliamentary terms are necessary, a glossary is included in the back of the book. It might be helpful to browse through it for unfamiliar terms before you begin reading.

As society becomes more complex, bureaucracy and organizations of all kinds burgeon. Meetings and their outcomes play an increasingly important role in our lives. Critical decision making occurs in meetings of committees, boards, and similar groups. Administrators, managers, businessmen, members of professional organizations, union members, and volunteers have never before had such overwhelming need for "meeting know-how."

This edition also contains a section on electronic meetings and their use. As the technology for electronic communication expands, organizations are increasingly using electronic means to communicate with members. Only one footnote and one paragraph are devoted to electronic meetings in the current edition of *Robert's Rules of Order Newly Revised.* Therefore, unlike the remainder of the book, the sections on electronic meetings are not based upon material specifically covered by *Robert's Rules.* Rather, they are the author's own guidelines for the democratic and parliamentary use of modern technology.

Throughout the book I will use examples of meetings of a fictitious community association I have called the Green Acres Association.

The use of the masculine has been employed for writing convenience only.

1

Parliamentary Procedure

1

How It All Began

Parliamentary procedure came to America with our ancestors. The term refers to the rules that have evolved over time to facilitate the democratic transaction of decision making in an organized group.

American parliamentary procedure is based on the procedural rules used in the English Parliament. Early American parliamentary procedure consisted of what the early settlers remembered of those rules. The complex system of English parliamentary law had developed over time in an awkward and unsystematized manner by a process of decisions and precedents.

It is no wonder the colonists had difficulty in remembering specific and intricate details.

At the time of the founding of our country, each colony had its own ideas of procedure. During the Continental Congress, each colony had different rules regarding how delegates were to be elected, the number of people they should represent, and so forth.

This confusing state of affairs continued until 1801. Thomas Jefferson, while serving as vice president, saw the need for a written and uniform system of rules. He compiled the *Manual of Parliamentary Practice,* which was immediately adopted by both the House and the Senate to prevent needless haggling over procedure.

At the same time, Americans began forming many different kinds of organizations—political, cultural, scientific, and so forth. Jefferson's manual was too complex and beyond the ability of the average citizen.

It was not until 1876 that Henry Martyn Robert, a practical, precise, and civic-minded engineer, put together a small book of rules specifically designed for nonlegislative organizations. He wrote that his parliamentary manual was "based, in its general principles, upon the rules and practices of Congress, and adapted in its details to the use of ordinary societies."

That first *Robert's Rules of Order* was an almost instant success. Groups who adopted it as a parliamentary authority were now free from the hassle of struggling with the rules governing their meetings.

Today we can be a part of any meeting in any state and know that the rules will be the same if *Robert's Rules of Order* is the adopted parliamentary authority. Motions are amended the same way whether the meeting takes place in California or in New York.

2

The Purpose of Parliamentary Procedure

Parliamentary law is the basis of all constitutional governments. By protecting and practicing correct parliamentary procedure, we also protect our democratic institutions. Parliamentary procedure protects the rights of people to join together to accomplish common goals and enables them to debate and take action in a fair manner with the least amount of controversy.

The rules of parliamentary procedure are based on common sense and logic. They have evolved throughout centuries of usage and custom. Parliamentary rules protect:

- the right of the majority to decide;
- the right of the minority to be heard;
- the rights of individual members; and
- the rights of absentees.

All of parliamentary procedure is built on the principle that there must be a careful balance of the rights of the organization as a whole, the rights of subgroups, and the rights of individual members.

Parliamentary procedure should be used to *help* and not *hinder* decision making. Robert said, "The assembly meets to transact business, not to have members exploit their knowledge of parliamentary law."

3

The Basic Rules of Parliamentary Procedure

The Rights of the Organization Supersede the Rights of Individual Members

The organization has the right to make its own rules, which then must be observed by all members. Should a conflict arise between the rights of a member and the right of the organization to do its business, the rights of the organization prevail.

Example

At a meeting of the Green Acres Association, a motion has been made that "a playground be constructed in the park area." Mrs. A has been recognized by the Chair and is speaking in favor of the motion. Mr. B, who is opposed to the motion, is calling out loud objections and engaging in argument with the speaker. The Chair calls the member to order. Mr. B continues his disruptive behavior, stating that as a member he has a "right" to speak. The Chair quietly states that the organization has the right to conduct business in an orderly manner, which supersedes the member's right to speak. The Chair further informs Mr. B that the organization has the right to eject any member who interferes with that right.

All Members Are Equal and Their Rights Are Equal

Those rights are:

- to attend meetings;
- to make motions and speak in debate;
- to nominate;
- to vote;
- to hold office.

Example

Mr. B has the right to voice his objections to the motion to construct a playground. However, he must seek recognition of the Chair and be recognized (assigned the floor) before he can speak in debate.

A Quorum Must Be Present to Do Business

A **quorum** is the number of members who must be present to legally transact business. The number is usually stated in the bylaws. In a committee or a small board, the quorum is the majority of its members. The purpose of a quorum is to prevent an unrepresentative group from taking action in the name of the organization.

Example

The hour is late and members have been steadily leaving the meeting of the Green Acres Association. A member moves "that a playground be constructed in the park area." A thoughtful member notices that the only members left are young couples with small children. He requests that the president determine the presence of a quorum. (The president could have taken this action without a request.) A quorum is not present and no action can be taken by the association on the matter of the playground.

The Majority Rules

This rule is basic to the democratic process. The minority has the right to be heard, but once a decision has been reached by a majority of the members present and voting, the minority must then respect and abide by the decision.

Example

A motion is made and adopted by a majority vote to postpone the motion to construct a playground until the next meeting. Mrs. A objects, stating that she will be out of town at the time of the next meeting. The Chair rules her objection out of order, reminding her that the majority of the members have voted to postpone.

Silence Is Consent

Those members who do not vote agree to go along with the decision of the majority by their silence.

Example

A special committee of seven has been appointed by the president to recommend a landscape architect to site the playground. Five members attend the meeting. (A majority being present, the committee has a quorum.) The choice has been narrowed to two landscape architects, one of whom is the committee chairman's brother-in-law. His name is presented first. Two members abstain from voting. The chairman and another vote for the brother-in-law, while the remaining member votes no. (The chairman of a committee actively participates in debate and votes.) The brother-in-law has been selected by a majority vote of the committee. Robert states that a majority means the majority of members voting. The abstentions do not count. Therefore, in a committee of seven, two votes determined the choice!

Two-Thirds Vote Rule

A **two-thirds vote** is necessary whenever you are limiting or taking away the rights of members or whenever you are changing something that has already been decided.

Example

The debate on the playground proposal has lasted an hour. A member moves **the previous question**.

(A motion to cut off debate and to vote immediately.) The motion is seconded. The president explains that the motion is not debatable and will require a two-thirds vote because it will cut off discussion. In other words, the group is taking away the right to debate.

One **Question at a Time and** ***One*** **Speaker at a Time**

No motion is in order which does not *directly relate* to the question under consideration. In addition, once a member has been recognized, he has been granted "the floor" and another member may not interrupt him.

Example

A motion has been made and seconded that the Green Acres Association construct a playground in the park area. Mr. G moves that the motion be amended to add "and that a perennial garden be planted at the entrance gates." The president rules the amendment out of order, explaining that the amendment does not relate to the issue of the playground. A gracious president might say, **"Would you hold that motion, Mr. G? The question on the floor at this time relates to the construction of a playground."** Had Mr. G interrupted a speaker, the president would have firmly informed him that another member had the floor and request that he wait for recognition before speaking.

Debatable Motions Must Receive Full Debate

The presiding officer may *not* put a debatable motion to vote as long as members wish to debate it. Debate can only be suspended by a two-thirds vote of the members present.

Example

The president has long felt the need for a community playground. The motion is made and seconded that a playground be constructed in the park area. He immediately states the question and asks for the ayes and nos. A member rises to a **point of order**, explaining that the motion is debatable and must receive full debate.

Once a Question Is Decided, It Is Not in Order to Bring Up the Same Motion or One Essentially Like It at the Same Meeting

Such motions should be ruled **out of order**. (Note: There is a special class of motions that do bring a motion back to the group, called **restorative motions**.)

Example

The association has voted to refer the selection of a landscape architect for site selection of the playground to a committee of seven. Mr. H moves that "Mr. W of European Designs be employed as the landscape architect." The president rules the motion out of order, as the matter has already been referred to a committee.

Personal Remarks In Debate Are Always Out of Order

The presiding officer must rule all personal remarks out of order. Debate must be directed to *motions* and not *motives; principles* and not *personalities.*

Example

Mrs. A has made a motion that a playground be constructed in the park area owned by the association. Mr. B rises and states that "Mrs. A is just another spoiled yuppie who should buy her own swing set!" The president quickly rules the remarks out of order, stating that debate must center on the motion and personal remarks about the member who made the motion are not in order.

These ten rules form the basis for all of the more specific material that follows.

II

What Officers Need to Know

4

Running a Meeting Effectively

The presiding officer, who carries the title of president or chairman, is responsible for maintaining order. He is much like a referee in a sports contest and has the responsibility of *enforcing* the rules in order that the organization may do its work in the fairest, most expedient and impartial manner. The degree of formality in presiding will depend on the size of the group and the amount of agreement in the group. A small group in close agreement needs less strict adherence to procedural rules than one in which sharp differences of opinion and warring cliques exist.

DUTIES OF A PRESIDING OFFICER

Be On Time and Start On Time!

The presiding officer should arrive early to check the readiness of the meeting room and should begin the meeting *promptly* at the scheduled hour if a quorum is present.

Example

On arriving fifteen minutes before the meeting, the president of the Green Acres Association noticed that the room was extremely warm and that there was insufficient seating for the number of members expected. He contacted the custodian to correct the situation.

At the appointed hour, the treasurer had not arrived, although the hall was filled with members. The president called the meeting to order at the scheduled time even though it might be necessary to amend the agenda to postpone the treasurer's report.

Be Organized

The presiding officer should have a detailed, well-prepared agenda and *stick* to it. (See "Preparing an Agenda," page 23.)

Example

The president has contacted those officers and chairmen with important reports to determine that they are prepared to report and has listed them on his written agenda.

Be Prepared

The presiding officer should be familiar with the procedural rules of the bylaws, the standing rules, and the customs of the group as well as the parliamentary authority.

Example

A member has made a motion that the members be assessed $100 to provide funds for construction of the playground. The presiding officer explains that the bylaws do not provide for the assessment of members; therefore, the motion is not in order.

Be a Teacher

The presiding officer should keep the group working together by explaining procedure clearly and communicating the next business in order. If a motion is confusing, it is his duty to clarify it. This may mean helping a member rephrase a motion or requiring a long motion to be submitted in writing.

Example

After the report of the officers, Mrs. A rises to speak about the need for a community playground. The presiding officer explains that the next business in order is committee reports and that new business will be announced.

When new business has been announced, Mrs. A again rises and begins a long diatribe about the children of the community having no place to play and that other communities are building playgrounds. The presiding officer interrupts to ask, **"Is it your intent to make a motion regarding a playground?"**

Be In Control of the Floor

The presiding officer should "assign" the floor by recognizing those members who wish to speak by calling them by name if possible.

No other member may interrupt or call out remarks without being out of order. The presiding officer should remind such a member that the floor has been assigned and request that his remarks be held until the floor has been assigned to him.

In addition, private discussion between members while another has the floor is out of order and disruptive members should be reminded of this rule.

Example

As the presiding officer calls on Mrs. A, there is rustling and giggling in the hall. Someone calls out, "Not the playground again!" Another member loudly states, "We'll be here all night."

The president firmly calls the meeting to order and reminds the group that Mrs. A has the floor, and those wishing to make comments will please wait until they have been assigned the floor.

Be Impartial

The presiding officer should call on members wishing to speak impartially. He should give members on both sides of an issue an opportunity to speak, calling the opposing sides of the motion alternately if possible.

Example
"Two members have spoken in favor of the motion. Is there a member who wishes to speak against the motion?"

Be Composed

The presiding officer should remain calm and objective, keeping the meeting moving. A sense of humor and a smile can often save the day!

Example
The discussion regarding construction of the playground has been heated. One member rises to state that families with children should be outlawed in Green Acres and that it should become an adult community. The presiding officer senses that the situation is volatile. If he can laugh and thank the member for his remark and move the meeting on to the next business at hand, he will avoid a public free-for-all.

Be Precise

The presiding officer should always *restate* the motion before taking a vote. After taking the vote, he *announces* the result of the vote by interpreting the action taken.

The presiding officer should always be certain about the results of a voice vote. He may retake the vote by requesting a rising vote or a show of hands on his own accord.

Example

"The question is on the construction of a playground in the community park. As many as are in favor please say aye. Those opposed will please say no. The chair is uncertain of the vote. Those in favor of constructing a playground in the community park will please rise. Thank you. Those opposed will please rise. Thank you. The nos have it, and a playground will not be constructed in the community park."

The members have literally seen the vote and are reassured that the presiding officer is correctly interpreting it.

Be Focused

The presiding officer should not allow irrelevant discussion. Restate the question and, if necessary, directly request the member to **"Confine his remarks to the motion on the floor."**

Example

Although the motion to construct a playground in the community park is on the floor, Mr. G and some of his friends continue to speak to the need for a perennial garden at the entrance gates. With a smile, the presiding officer says, **"The chair is aware of the feelings of some of the members regarding a garden at the entrance gates. However, the motion on the floor pertains to the construction of a playground. Please confine all discussion to the motion that is before us."**

Be Temperate

The presiding officer should use the gavel *sparingly*, tapping it once to open and close the meeting.

Example

It is the presiding officer who sets the example of courtesy and of operating within the rules. If the meeting seems to be out of order, firmly call the members to order and stand quietly until you have their attention. Never try to shout over a din. Avoid the gavel pounding that we have witnessed in national political conventions.

Always remember that informality should not equate with chaos!

PREPARING AN AGENDA

- An agenda is an outline of a meeting. It is a list of things to be acted upon or information to be given.
- The use of an agenda form that lists the standard order of business is helpful. (See "A Suggested Form for an Agenda," page 24.)
- Officers and committees to report are listed in the order in which they appear in the bylaws. Special or ad hoc committees follow standing committees.
- List only those officers or chairmen whom you know to have reports. At the conclusion of the reports known to you ask, **"Are there other offi-**

cers with reports?" This not only saves time but also prevents the organization from appearing to be a "do nothing" one by omitting **"No report"** responses.

- Check the bylaws for requirements that certain business be conducted at specific meetings of the year.

Examples

- Appointment of auditors
- Adoption of the auditor's report
- Election of a nominating committee
- Election of delegates and alternates

- Check the minutes of the last meeting for any business that was postponed.
- Boards with a heavy schedule of business may require a **circulated agenda** with reproduced material enclosed to provide background information to prepare members for decision making.

A Suggested Form for an Agenda

I. Call to Order
II. Opening Ceremonies (optional)
  A. Welcoming remarks
  B. Invocation (God first)
  C. Pledge of Allegiance (country after God)
III. Minutes of the Previous Meeting
IV. Reports of the Officers
  A. Report of the Treasurer
V. Report of the Executive Board (annual meeting)

VI. Reports of Standing Committees
VII. Reports of Special Committees
VIII. Special Orders
IX. Unfinished Business and General Orders
  A. Do not use the archaic term "old" business. This refers to business brought over from the previous meeting.
X. New Business
XI. Announcements or Program
XII. Adjournment

SCRIPT FOR A PRESIDING OFFICER

CALL TO ORDER: (First determine the presence of a quorum.) **"Good evening. A quorum being present, the meeting will come to order."** (Stand quietly, *do not* pound your gavel. One rap will suffice.)

MINUTES: **"The first business in order is the approval of the minutes of the previous meeting. Will Mrs. B please read the minutes of the last meeting?** [Example of **general consent**] **Are there any corrections to the minutes?** [Pause.] **There being no corrections, the minutes are approved as read** (*or* **as circulated**)." (If there are corrections, the corrections are noted and made by the secretary at this time.) **"The minutes are approved as corrected."**

REPORTS OF THE OFFICERS: **"The next business in order will be the reports of the officers."** (Call on only those officers you know to have reports, using the order as listed in the bylaws.)

TREASURER'S REPORT: **"The treasurer,** [call by name], **will give his report."**

"Are there any questions? [Pause.] **There being none, the report will be filed for audit."** (Do *not* **adopt** the treasurer's report. The auditor's report is adopted at the annual meeting.) **"Are there other officers with reports?"**

COMMITTEE REPORTS: **"There being none, the next business in order will be the reports of committees."** (Call on standing committees first in the order as listed in the bylaws, then special committees.)

Example: Mr. K, chairman of the extension committee, will now report. (Do *not* adopt the report; file it with the minutes of the meeting.) **"Thank you, Mr. K. The report will be filed with the minutes of this meeting."** (If the report contains specific recommendations for action, they should be put into the form of a motion and acted upon.)

SPECIAL ORDERS: (Matters that the bylaws require action on at a specific meeting, such as the election of a nominating committee.)

UNFINISHED BUSINESS: (Do *not* announce unless the minutes show that business has been postponed to this meeting.) **"The next business in order will be the proposed bylaw amendments that were postponed to this meeting. Mr. M, the bylaws chairman, will please report."**

NEW BUSINESS: **"The next business in order will be new business. Is there any new business to come before the group?"**

ANNOUNCEMENTS OR PROGRAM: **"If there is no further new business to come before the group, the secretary will read the announcements."**

Or

"Mr. P, the program chairman, will introduce the speaker of the day."

ADJOURNMENT: (Use general consent.) **"If there is no further business and there is no objection, the meeting will be adjourned.** [Pause.] **There being no objection, the meeting is adjourned."**

PARLIAMENTARY TECHNIQUES TO EXPEDITE BUSINESS

Use General Consent When Possible

Voting takes time. When business is routine or when the group is in agreement, a formal vote or a formal motion may be unnecessary.

Example

"If there is no objection, we will recess for ten minutes while the ballots are counted. [Pause to see if any member objects.] **There being no objection, we will recess for ten minutes."**

If there is a *single* objection, the matter must be put to a vote.

Example

A member states, **"I object!"** The presiding officer then states the question. **"An objection being made, the question is shall we recess for ten minutes? As many as are in favor, say aye. Those opposed, say no. The ayes have it, and we will recess for ten minutes."**

General consent may also be used with amendments to motions if the Chair feels the group will accept the amendment.

Example

A motion has been made at the Green Acres Association that a playground be constructed in the community park. Mrs. A moves that the motion be amended to include the words "with the surplus in the maintenance fund." After discussion, it appears clear to the presiding officer that the group feels the surplus in the maintenance fund should be used for the project. The presiding officer states, **"If there is no objection, the motion will be amended to include**

the words 'with the surplus in the maintenance fund.' [Pause.] **There being no objection, the motion is so amended.** [Restate motion as amended.] **The motion is that 'a playground be constructed in the community park with the surplus in the maintenance fund.'"**

General consent is permitted by the parliamentary principle that rules are designed to protect the right of the majority to decide and the right of the minority to be heard. Therefore, when there is consensus among the group and no minority to protect, the rules do not need to be as strictly enforced.

Elections May Be by Acclamation

When only one candidate is proposed for each position on a slate of officers and no further nominations are made from the floor, the presiding officer may declare the slate elected by **acclamation** unless the bylaws require a ballot vote.

Example

Officers are to be elected at the annual meeting of the Green Acres Association. The presiding officer calls for the report of the nominating committee. The chairman of the committee names one nominee for each position. The president thanks the nominating committee and calls for nominations from the floor for president, vice president, and so on. There are no nominations from the floor. The president then says, **"There being no further nominations from the floor, I**

declare the slate presented by the nominating committee to be elected by acclamation."

Assist Members in Phrasing Motions

A member may request the floor and begin discussion of a subject without making a motion. The Chair may tactfully interrupt the dialogue by helping the member to frame a motion.

Example

Mr. G of the Green Acres Association rises, and on being recognized begins a speech about the need for healthy outdoor activities for children. He states that other communities are building playgrounds and Green Acres has no sidewalks or places for the children to play.

The president tactfully interrupts and asks, **"Is it your intent, Mr. G, to make a motion that the Green Acres Association construct a playground?"**

If Mr. G agrees, there is a clear motion on the floor.

Or:

The president might assume a motion from Mr. G by stating after his speech, **"The question is whether the Green Acres Association shall construct a playground."**

In either case, the association has benefited from a good presiding officer who is attempting to keep discussion focused and to expedite action in the meeting.

Restate the Motion on the Floor Whenever Discussion Is Wandering from the Subject

Example

The question on the floor is the construction of a playground in the community park. Mrs. G rises and states that the community entrance is unattractive. Mr. B rises and states that the gates should be functional. The presiding officer should restate the question: **"The motion on the floor is the construction of a playground in the community park. Members will please direct their remarks to that question."**

ALLOW THE WITHDRAWAL OF MOTIONS

After some discussion, the maker of the motion may realize that he has made a poor motion and request that it be withdrawn. General consent is used to withdraw the motion. The permission of the seconder is *not* needed. A withdrawn motion does not appear in the minutes. It is as if the motion had never been made.

Example

Mrs. E makes the motion that "the association assess members $100 for construction of the playground." During discussion it is brought out that the bylaws do not provide for assessment and that the maintenance fund has a surplus. Mrs. E realizes she has made a poor motion and asks that her motion be withdrawn. The presiding officer says, **"If there is no objection, the**

motion will be withdrawn. [Pause.] **There being no objection, the motion is withdrawn."**

A Consent Agenda May Be Used for Noncontroversial Business

A **consent agenda** disposes of a number of matters at one time without taking separate action on each one. It is used to provide more time for important business by taking action on noncontroversial items with a single vote.

A consent agenda is drawn up by the president and professional staff. It is a list of routine business that requires action but not necessarily discussion. These items may all be approved at the same time by either a majority vote or general consent.

Examples of Items for a Consent Agenda

- Confirm the appointment of Mr. X as the Green Acres representative to the county Planning Council
- Confirm appointment of committee members (list the names and the committees)
- Approve ordering office stationery
- Accept the resignation of Mr. W.

Any member may ask that any listed item be removed from the consent agenda. That item is then placed on the regular agenda and handled in the usual way.

DILATORY TACTICS

A **dilatory tactic** is the *misuse* of a parliamentary procedure to deliberately delay or prevent action in a meeting. Every group has the right to protect itself from such tactics.

It is the duty of the presiding officer to prevent a dissident minority from misusing legitimate forms of motions to obstruct business. Such motions should be ruled out of order or those members engaged in such game playing should not be recognized.

Examples of Dilatory Tactics

- Members who constantly demand a recount using **division** (which requires a revote) on every vote when the results are perfectly clear to all the members
- A small group of members who repeatedly raise points of order or **appeal** the Chair's decisions
- Motions that are foolish, with clear intent to delay action

5

The Secretary and Minute Keeping

The secretary is responsible for the minutes of an organization, both the meetings of the membership and those of the executive board. Minutes are a written record of the meetings. Accurate minutes are of vital importance as they constitute the permanent record of proposals, decisions, and reports of the members and the executive board. Minutes are the *legal* record of the meetings of an organization and may be subpoenaed. Minutes should be written as concisely as possible.

A GUIDE FOR WRITING MINUTES

Do Record

- All adopted and "lost" or defeated motions
- Name of the maker of the motion

- Names of all members reporting (officers, committee chairmen, etc.)
- Names of all those elected or appointed
- Number of votes on each side in a ballot or counted vote

Don't Record

- Discussion or personal opinion
- Name of the seconder of a motion
- Motions withdrawn
- Entire reports (state, **"Mr. Y, chairman of the personnel policy committee, reported. The report is attached to the original of these minutes."**)

Important Points

- Write the minutes as promptly as possible. Your notes will be easier to decipher.
  A. Promptly send a copy to the president.
  B. Alert the president to items of unfinished business.
- Prepare a summary of the executive board meetings and be prepared to report motions to the membership.
- Sign the minutes and record the date of approval.
- Be specific in recording corrections, noting the date, page, and line in which the correction appears. All corrections are made in red. Do not obliterate the original. Note the date of the correction. Minutes are usually corrected at the time of the reading but may be cor-

rected at any time provided the correction receives a two-thirds vote. (Remember that you are changing something already adopted, which requires a two-thirds vote.)

CONTENTS OF MINUTES

First Paragraph

- Kind of meeting (regular or special)
- Name of the organization
- Date and place of meeting
- Presence of the president and the secretary or the names of the substitutes
- Presence of a quorum
- Time the meeting was called to order
- Whether the minutes of the previous meeting were approved or corrected

Example

(Name of the organization)

Minutes

A (regular) meeting of the (name of the organization) was held on (date) at (place). The president and secretary were present. (Or: The vice president, (name), presided in the absence of the president.) A quorum being present, the meeting was called to order at (time). The minutes of the previous meeting were approved as read (Or: as corrected).

Body

- Reports given, including:
  A. the name of the reporter;
  B. any related action taken.
- All main motions (those that propose action be taken).
- All points of order or appeal.
- Important announcements, such as the topic of the program and the name of the speaker (do *not* try to summarize the address).

Example

The treasurer's report showed a balance on hand of $____. The report was filed for audit.

____, chairman of the ____ committee, reported. The report is filed with the minutes of this meeting. At the conclusion of the report, the chairman moved the adoption of the following resolution:

Whereas, The ____; be it

RESOLVED, That ____.

The resolution was adopted.

Under Unfinished Business, the motion postponed to this meeting "That ____" was lost [or defeated].

Under New Business, a motion by ____ was amended and adopted as follows:

"____."

The program was given by ____, who spoke on the subject of ____.

Final Paragraph

The adjournment and the time of adjournment.

Example

The meeting was adjourned at (time).
(signature of secretary)
(date)
Approved,
[or:]
Corrected: (date)

OTHER DUTIES OF THE SECRETARY

The secretary is also the official keeper of the records of the organization, which include:

- the official membership roll;
- a list of all committees and their members; and
- a current copy of the bylaws with any amendments noted and any special rules adopted by the organization.

In the event of a roll call vote, the secretary assists by calling each member's name and recording his vote.

The secretary is also responsible for sending out notices of meetings and other correspondence unless the organization has a corresponding secretary.

6

The Treasurer and His Duties

The treasurer is responsible for the funds of the organization. He receives and disburses the monies as prescribed in the bylaws and as directed by the membership. In addition, he usually bills for and collects the annual dues.

He maintains a permanent record book with a detailed account of all money received and all money paid out. Corrections should be clearly indicated in red and never erased. The treasurer is also responsible for any federal, state, or local taxes and the timely filing of required tax forms.

The treasurer should give a *brief* report at each meeting. This report should be a summary of the collections and expenditures, calling attention to any unusual items.

The treasurer's report is *not* adopted. The presiding officer should allow questions and then state that the report will be filed for audit. (Note: Members could not possibly do sums in their heads, nor verify bills.) The annual auditor's report, which checks and verifies the accuracy of the books, is voted on.

The books of the treasurer should be audited annually prior to the treasurer's annual report. Small organizations unable to incur the expense of an auditing firm may appoint an auditing committee of its members to review the books. A notation is made in the ledger to show that the books have been audited.

Audited, (date), (signature of the chairman)

An audit report is prepared to reflect the findings and recommendations of the committee. If no irregularities or errors are found, the report states:

The books of (name of organization) were audited and found correct.

The report is dated and signed by the chairman and all of the members of the committee.

The treasurer may also be responsible for the preparation of a **budget**, which is an itemized summary of anticipated income and expenses for the upcoming fiscal or administrative year. The budget is prepared based on experience and data as recorded in the financial records. The bylaws prescribe whether the budget is adopted by the executive board or the membership. The budget is adopted at the annual meeting of the specified group. It is open to amendment at that time. If it becomes necessary to amend the budget later in the year, the amendment requires a two-thirds vote or **previous notice** and a majority vote.

It is generally agreed that organizations should maintain a separate investment fund that is equal to six months of the operating budget.

A SAMPLE FORM FOR A TREASURER'S REPORT

(date)

Receipts

Balance on hand (date of last meeting):$1,000.00

Dues: 100 members at $1.00,	$100.00
Donations:	$100.00
RECEIPTS	$200.00
TOTAL	$1,200.00

Disbursements

Per capita dues: 100 members at $0.50

National organization:	$50.00
Postage:	$25.00
TOTAL	$75.00

Reserve Funds

—

Balance on Hand (Date of Report)

$1,125.00

(Signature of treasurer)

III

Motions and Their Use

7

Types of Motions

Motions are the tools used to introduce business in a meeting. No business can be introduced without a motion. There are two kinds of motions: **main motions** and **secondary motions**.

MAIN MOTIONS

A main motion is defined as a proposal that certain action be taken or an opinion be expressed by the group. Main motions allow a group to do its work. They are the motions that spend money, adopt projects, and so forth. The words to use are **"I move."**

Example

"I move that a playground be constructed in the community park with the surplus in the maintenance fund."

SECONDARY MOTIONS

A secondary motion is one that can be made *while* the main motion is on the floor and before it has been decided.

Example

"I move that the motion to construct a playground be referred to a special committee of five to be appointed by the president."

Secondary motions are divided into three classes which relate to their use in parliamentary procedure. Those classes are **subsidiary motions**, **privileged motions**, and **incidental motions**.

Subsidiary Motions

Subsidiary motions relate directly to the motion on the floor. They may change the words, send it to a committee, delay it, and so on. They are designed to expedite business by disposing of the pending motion other than by adopting or rejecting it. Subsidiary motions are the class of motions most frequently used in meetings.

Subsidiary motions cause confusion because they have **rank** among themselves. Robert calls rank "the order of precedence of motions." A motion of higher rank can be made while a motion of lower rank is on the floor. The motion of lower rank "yields" to the one of higher rank.

Example
A member rises and says, **"I move that the question of constructing a playground be postponed until the next meeting as the hour is late."**

The subsidiary motion to **postpone** has higher rank than the motion to **commit** and takes precedence. The presiding officer takes the vote on postponing the question. If the motion to postpone is adopted, the main motion and the motion to commit are postponed until the next meeting.

Privileged Motions

Privileged motions are motions of an emergency nature, such as to recess or adjourn. They do not relate to the motion on the floor but to the welfare of the group. They are of high rank and must be handled before any other business that may be pending.

Example
The motion to construct a playground is on the floor. A member notices that it is 12:30 p.m. and the hotel has been instructed to serve lunch at that time. He rises and says, **"I move that we recess for lunch."** The motion to recess is a privileged motion and takes precedence over the main motion to construct a playground.

Incidental Motions

Incidental motions are procedural. They deal with process, such as enforcing proper procedure, correcting errors, verifying votes, and so on. When introduced, they must be decided before business can resume.

Example

A concerned member notices that feeling regarding the playground is so intense and divided that a secret vote would be in the best interests of the group. He rises and says, **"I move that the vote be by ballot."** The group must stop and vote on the incidental motion to vote by ballot.

Robert's Rules in Plain English, Second Edition, will present only those subsidiary, privileged, and incidental motions that are the most commonly used. The current edition of *Robert's Rules of Order Newly Revised* deals in detail with all motions.

You will find that some motions are debatable, others are not; some may be amended, others may not. Some motions require a majority vote to adopt, others a two-thirds vote. These points are known as the "Standard Characteristics" of a motion.

HOW A MOTION IS MADE AND ACTED UPON

The Steps to Obtain Action

A MEMBER REQUESTS THE FLOOR

The member rises and addresses the Chair: **"Mr. President."**

THE FLOOR IS ASSIGNED

The Chair recognizes the member and assigns him the floor by calling his name if possible, **"Mr. G."** Personal recognition helps keep order by informing the group that Mr. G has the floor.

THE MOTION IS MADE

Mr. G introduces the motion by saying, **"I move . . . "** For example, **"I move that the association construct a playground in the community park with the surplus in the maintenance fund."**

THE MOTION IS SECONDED

Another member says, **"I second the motion."** This member does *not* need to rise and does not wait to be recognized.

Why a second? Robert says that a motion must be considered if two people are in favor of its coming before the meeting.

Motions from a committee do *not* need a second as the group knows that at least two people want it considered.

If a motion fails to get a second, the Chair states, **"Since there is no second, the motion is not before this meeting."**

THE CHAIR STATES THE MOTION

It is important that the Chair restate the motion so that the proposal is clarified in the minds of the members. **"It has been moved and seconded that the association construct a playground in the community**

park with the surplus in the maintenance fund." This also serves to keep the members focused and discussion centered on the construction of a playground.

The Chair can always require that a long and involved motion be submitted in writing so that he can accurately restate it.

The motion is said to be **pending** once it has been stated by the Chair. It must be disposed of in some manner before other business can be considered.

DEBATE IS HELD

The Chair opens debate by saying, **"Is there any discussion?"** The Chair must open all debatable questions to debate.

The Chair recognizes members who wish to speak by stating their names. In a large group in which members may be unknown to the Chair, the member is asked to identify himself. Members quickly establish the habit of waiting to be recognized by the Chair before speaking.

Debate should continue as long as members wish to discuss the question unless motions have been adopted to either limit or close debate.

THE CHAIR PUTS THE QUESTION TO A VOTE

The vote is taken in the following way:

1. The Chair again restates the motion. **"The question is on the motion that the association construct a playground in the community park with the surplus in the maintenance fund."**

Restating the motion keeps the members clear about the purpose of the vote.

2. **"All in favor of the motion please say aye . . . those opposed say no."**

This is an example of a **voice vote.**

THE CHAIR ANNOUNCES THE VOTE

The Chair interprets and announces the results of the vote. **"The nos have it, and the association will not construct a playground in the community park."**

The Chair is explaining the outcome of the vote to the members.

RULES THAT GOVERN MAIN MOTIONS

Rules Regarding Main Motions

- Cannot interrupt a member who has been assigned the floor
- Require a second, unless the motion is from a committee
- Can be debated
- Can be amended
- Require a majority vote

Other Points

- The Chair can require a long motion to be submitted in writing.
- The maker of a motion has first right to speak to it.
- A member can vote against his own motion, but cannot speak against it.

- A member can modify his own motion before it is stated by the Chair. The member can also offer an amendment after his motion has been stated by the Chair.
- A member can withdraw his motion up to the time it has been stated by the Chair, and after that he must have permission of the group.

Motions That the Chair Should Rule Out of Order

- Motions that conflict with the law or with the bylaws
- Motions that repeat the same question on the same day
- Motions that conflict with an already adopted motion
- Motions that operate outside the scope or object of the organization
- Motions that conflict with or repeat motions held in committee
- Motions that appear dilatory, incorrect, frivolous, or rude

8

Subsidiary Motions and Rank

Subsidiary motions have **rank** among each other. They are arranged in a specific order in which they must be considered and acted upon, some motions taking precedence over others. The purpose is to avoid confusion when they are applied to a main motion.

Rank means that a motion of **higher rank** can be made at the time that a motion of **lower rank** is on the floor or **pending**. A motion of higher rank **takes precedence** over a motion of lower rank.

Common sense dictates this rule. It is a waste of time to discuss an amendment to a motion if the group may decide to send that motion to a committee for study. Consequently, the motion to commit has precedence over the motion to amend.

There is a common misconception that a group cannot have two motions on the floor at the same time. More than one motion can be on the floor but only *one question*. All of the pending motions must relate to the main motion on the floor. No new business may be introduced.

For example, the motion that the association construct a playground is on the floor. Subsidiary motions to amend the motion, send it to a committee for study, or postpone it are in order. All of these motions relate to the main motion about constructing a playground, and they all have rank among themselves.

No new motion that does not directly relate to the question of the playground construction can be considered. For example, a motion to plant a perennial garden at the entrance introduces an entirely new question. It is a **main motion** and takes precedence over nothing. Main motions occupy the bottom rung of the ladder.

The simplest way to understand rank is to imagine the subsidiary motions making up the rungs of a stepladder. Those motions on the lower rungs must yield to the motions on the rung or rungs above. For instance, **previous question** (to call for an immediate vote) is near the top rung of the ladder. This motion takes precedence over all the motions that are lower on the ladder. This means that previous question can be made even if there are motions to amend, commit, or the like attached to the main motion regarding the construction of a playground. Previous question has the highest rank and is decided first.

Please study the stepladder chart for the ranking or order of precedence of the subsidiary motions.

THE RANK OF MOTIONS IS LIKE A STEPLADDER.

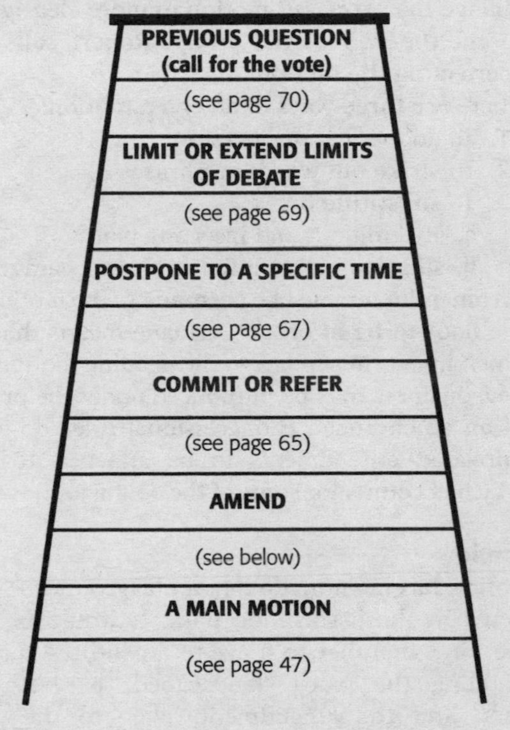

AMEND

Amend is the most frequently used and most important of the subsidiary motions. Amend can also cause the most confusion in groups.

- To amend a motion means to change the wording of a motion to make it clearer, more complete, or more acceptable *before* the motion is voted upon.

The amending process allows the group to change the proposed motion to more clearly represent the will of the group. Robert calls this "perfecting the motion."

- There are three ways to amend a motion:
    1. To add words or phrases
    2. To strike out words or phrases
    3. To substitute by:
        a. striking out and inserting words
        b. substituting an entire motion or paragraph
- An amendment must be **germane** to the motion on the floor to be in order. Germane means that the amendment must relate to the pending motion. No new business may be introduced under the pretext of an amendment. (Congressional rules do allow unrelated amendments to be attached to bills which accounts for some of the confusion.)

Example

A motion has been made that a playground be constructed in the association park. It would be germane for a member to move to amend the motion by adding the word "landscaped" as both the motion and the amendment relate to the playground. However, an amendment to add "and a perennial garden be planted at the entrance" is not in order as it is not germane. The second amendment relates to the entrance gate rather than to the playground and must be a separate question.

- A frequent point of confusion in the amending process is the misconception that there can be only one motion on the floor at a time. The rule is: There can be only *one question* on the floor at a time.

- Adoption of the amendment *does not adopt the motion*. The group has simply changed the motion on the floor. The motion may be amended further.

  If the group votes no on the amendment, the motion is on the floor as it was originally worded.

Example

The motion on the floor of the Green Acres Association is that a playground be constructed in the community park. Mrs. G rises and moves **"That the motion be amended by adding the words 'in the southeast corner' after the word 'constructed.'"** The amendment is seconded and discussed. The presiding officer puts the question on the amendment. **"The question is on the amendment to add the words 'in the southeast corner' after the word 'constructed.' As many as are in favor say aye. Those opposed say no. The nos have it and the amendment is lost. The question is shall the association construct a playground in the community park."**

- An amendment may also be amended.
- The first amendment is called a **primary amendment** and the amendment to the amendment is called a **secondary amendment**.
- Only two amendments may be pending at any

one time. In other words, an amendment to an amendment to an amendment is not in order; otherwise, the group would become hopelessly confused.

- The presiding officer is like a referee. He must know the rules and be able to guide the group so that the members know what is going on, where they are, and what they may properly do.

The Process of Amending an Amendment

FIRST VOTE ON
The **amendment to the amendment** (the secondary amendment).

NEXT VOTE ON
The **original amendment** (the primary amendment).

FINALLY VOTE ON
The **main motion** (which may or may not have been amended).

Example

There is a motion on the floor of the Green Acres Association that **"A playground be constructed in the community park with the surplus in the maintenance fund."**

An amendment has been offered to insert the words **"fenced"** before the word **"playground."** The amendment is seconded and is discussed.

An amendment to the amendment is offered to

strike out the word **"fenced"** and insert the word **"landscaped."** The amendment is seconded and discussed.

The presiding officer takes the following action:

1. **"The question is on the amendment to the amendment, to strike out the word 'fenced' and insert the word 'landscaped.' As many as are in favor of the amendment to the amendment, say aye. Those opposed say no. The ayes have it."**
2. **"The question now on the floor is that the word 'landscaped' be inserted before the word 'playground' in the motion that a playground be constructed in the community park with the surplus in the maintenance fund. As many as are in favor of the amendment say aye; those opposed, no. The ayes have it."**
3. **"The question now on the floor is that the association construct a landscaped playground in the community park with the surplus in the maintenance fund."**
4. The motion may be further amended at this point.
5. A member may move to further amend the motion by adding the words **"in the southeast corner"** before the words **"community park."** The presiding officer follows the same process, stating the question, allowing debate, and taking the vote on the amendment. If this amendment is adopted, the motion on the floor now is **"that a landscaped playground be constructed in the southeast**

corner of the community park with the surplus in the maintenance fund."

- A motion may also be amended by substituting an entirely new motion for the motion on the floor, provided that it is germane. This can be a valuable tool in offering an acceptable compromise to an unacceptable motion on the floor.

Example

Mr. K rises and says, **"I move to amend the motion by substituting 'that Creative Playgrounds be asked to present a proposal with cost estimates for the construction of a playground.'"**

- There are special rules the presiding officer must know to handle a substitute amendment.

  A = MAIN MOTION
  B = SUBSTITUTE MOTION

  1. Motion A is stated and is allowed to be further amended.
  2. Motion B is next stated and amendments are also allowed.
  3. The vote is taken on whether Motion B will be substituted for Motion A.

Example

The presiding officer states that the motion has been made to substitute **"that Creative Playgrounds be asked to present a proposal with cost estimates for the construction of a playground"** for the motion

"that a landscaped playground be constructed in the southeast corner of the community park with the surplus in the maintenance fund."

(The presiding officer needs to explain to the group the process of amending.)

"Our parliamentary authority, *Robert's Rules of Order,* states that when a motion is made to amend by substitution, we first go back to the original motion and allow the friends of it to further amend it. Next we take the substitute and open it up for discussion and amendment. The last step is the vote on whether you wish to substitute or not."

---

1. **"The original motion is that a landscaped playground be constructed in the southeast corner of the community park with the surplus in the maintenance fund. Is there any further discussion or amendment?"**
2. **"The question is now on the substitute, that Creative Playgrounds be asked to present a proposal with cost estimates for the construction of a playground. Is there any discussion or amendment?"**
3. **"The question is now on substituting the motion that Creative Playgrounds be asked to present a proposal with cost estimates for the construction of a playground for the motion that a landscaped playground be constructed in the southeast corner of the community park with the surplus in the maintenance fund."**

4. **"As many as are in favor of substituting say aye. Those opposed say no. The ayes have it and the motion is substituted."**

- The reader will be happy to learn that the substitute motion may only be further amended by adding at the end. It must still be voted on by the group. They have only voted to *substitute* and not to *adopt*.

Parliamentary Rules of Amendments

- A member must obtain the floor to offer an amendment; a speaker cannot be interrupted.
- An amendment must be seconded.
- It is debatable, if the amendment is made to a debatable motion.
- It can be amended. (A secondary amendment cannot be amended.)
- It requires a majority vote even if it is applied to a motion that requires a two-thirds vote.

A FRIENDLY AMENDMENT

A friendly amendment may be defined as a change in the wording that enhances and strengthens the original motion. When such a change is proposed and no one objects, the amendment may be adopted by general consent.

A HOSTILE AMENDMENT

A hostile amendment may be defined as one that gives a very different meaning to a motion. The amendment may defeat the intent of the main motion.

Example

A motion is on the floor to commend the president. It may be amended by striking out "commend " and inserting the word "censure." The amendment is *germane* because both commend and censure refer to the opinion the group has of the president.

AMENDMENTS THAT ARE OUT OF ORDER

Those amendments are out of order which:

- do not relate to the motion (are not germane);
- are the same as a negative vote on the motion;
- are dilatory or foolish; and
- would make the motion incoherent.

COMMIT

To **commit** or **refer** a motion sends the question on the floor to a small number of people so that it can be carefully studied and put into proper form for the group to consider.

This is a very useful motion when all of the facts may not be known. It prevents long and pointless debate and protects the group from making a poor decision.

For example, in the case of constructing a playground in the park of the Green Acres Association a committee might:

- survey the members to determine the need;
- discover whether the city would provide matching funds; and
- obtain cost estimates, etc.

Give Direction to the Motion

The motion should include specific directions as to where the question is to go and should address the following questions:

- A standing committee or a new special committee?
- What size committee?
- How shall the committee be selected?
- Will the committee have authority?
- When shall the committee report?

Example

"I move that the question of constructing a playground be referred to a committee of five, to be appointed by the president with instructions to report back at our next meeting."

The presiding officer is often faced with an incomplete motion such as **"I move that we refer the motion to a committee."**

He should help the member complete the motion by asking the member, **"To what committee shall the matter be referred?"**

If the answer is **"a special or ad hoc committee,"** he proceeds to ask how many members will the committee have, how they are to be selected, and when the committee should report.

Parliamentary Rules of Commit

- The motion to commit can be applied to any main motion *with any amendments* that may be pending. The amendments go *with* the motion to the committee.
- It must be seconded.
- It can be debated. However, *debate can only go into the desirability of committing and not into the main question*. For example, the advisability of constructing the playground cannot be debated.
- It can be amended as to which committee, what size committee, the instructions, etc.
- It requires a majority vote.

POSTPONE

The motion to **postpone** delays action on a question until later in the same meeting or until the next meeting. A motion *cannot* be postponed further than the next regular meeting; however, it may be **renewed** at a later date.

How the Motion Is Used

Postpone is useful when:

- an invited speaker/dignitary has arrived;
- information regarding the pending motion will be available later in the meeting;

- a member realizes his delegation is not present for the vote; and
- it is time for a recess or adjournment.

Parliamentary Rules of Postpone

- Postpone can be applied to all main motions.
- It must be seconded.
- It cannot interrupt a speaker.
- It can be debated; however, debate can only go into the desirability of postponing and not into the main question.
- It can be amended as to the time of the postponement; however, it cannot be postponed beyond the next regular business meeting or the end of the session in an annual convention.
- It requires a majority vote.

The motion is called up automatically when the time to which it was postponed arrives. If the motion was postponed until the next meeting, the presiding officer will schedule the motion on the agenda under **unfinished business**.

Example

At the meeting of the Green Acres Association, Mr. B rises and says, **"As the hour is late, I move that the motion regarding the construction of a playground be postponed until the next meeting."** If the motion is seconded and adopted, the president will schedule the motion and any amendments adhering to it under unfinished business for the next meeting.

LIMIT DEBATE

Limit debate is the motion by which the group can exercise special control over debate by:

- Reducing the number and length of speeches allowed

Example
"I move that debate on the construction of the playground be limited to one speech of two minutes for each member."

- Requiring that debate be limited to a period of time, at the end of which the vote must be taken

Example
"I move that at 9:00 p.m. debate be closed and the question on the playground be put to a vote."

This motion is seldom used in regular meetings. It is helpful where the size of the group or the volume of business indicates that the meeting will be too lengthy.

Parliamentary Rules of Limit Debate

- Limit debate can be used with any motion.
- It must be seconded.
- It cannot interrupt a speaker.
- It is not debatable.

- It can be amended, but only as to the length of speeches or when the vote will be taken.
- It requires a two-thirds vote because it takes away the rights of members.
- The vote may not be taken by voice but must be taken by a show of hands in a small group or a rising vote in a large group.

HINT

A timekeeper and a timer are necessary if speeches have a time limit. After the motion is adopted, the presiding officer appoints a member to keep time. **"The motion to limit speeches to two minutes has been adopted. The Chair appoints Mrs. X to serve as timekeeper."**

An electronic timer makes a nice little noise to alert the speaker and presiding officer that the time is up. It may be necessary for the presiding officer to politely remind the speaker, **"Your time is up."**

PREVIOUS QUESTION

Previous question is the motion used to cut off debate and to bring the group to an immediate vote on the pending motion (the motion on the floor that was stated last).

Example

"I move the previous question."

- It is rude to call out **"Question!"** and the presiding officer should ignore such calls.
- Previous question can be ruled out of order if the motion is debatable and has not received debate.
- The presiding officer should explain the effect of the motion to the members and clarify whether the motion is to apply to all the motions on the floor.

Example

"The previous question has been moved. This is a motion to stop debate and vote immediately. This motion requires a two-thirds vote. As many as are in favor will please rise. Thank you. Those opposed will please rise. Thank you. There being two-thirds in favor, we will vote on the motion to construct a playground in the southeast corner of the community park."

Parliamentary Rules of Previous Question

- Previous question can be applied to any pending question.
- It is out of order when a member has the floor.
- It cannot be debated.
- It requires a two-thirds vote because the right of members to debate is being curtailed.
- Because it requires a two-thirds vote, the vote must be taken by a show of hands in a small group or a rising vote in a large group.

CONCLUSION OF SUBSIDIARY MOTIONS

Subsidiary motions are always considered in order of their rank or order of precedence. (Review the stepladder chart on page 57.) When a subsidiary motion is pending, any motion above it in rank is in order; any motion below it in rank is out of order.

Example

- It has been moved that the motion regarding the construction of a playground be referred to an ad hoc committee of five to be appointed by the president and to report back at the next meeting.
- The motion to amend is out of order. It is of lower rank than commit. Practically speaking, why should the group waste time amending a motion that is going to a committee for study?
- The motion to postpone is in order. It is of higher rank than commit. It might serve the interests of the group to postpone the entire question until the next meeting. (Perhaps tempers are hot and the group hopelessly divided. Time can often soften and heal.)

Chart 1 is arranged by the rank of motions and lists the purpose of the motion, the parliamentary name of the motion, what to say to introduce it, and the vote required to adopt it.

CHART 1 **WHAT DO I SAY?**
Subsidiary Motions from Lowest to Highest Rank

TO DO THIS	MOTION	YOU SAY THIS	VOTE REQUIRED
Introduce Business	Main	**"I move that . . ."**	Majority
Change the Wording of a Motion	Amend	**"I move to amend the motion by . . ."** (adding words; striking out or substituting words)	Majority
Send to Committee	Commit	**"I move that the motion be referred to . . ."**	Majority
Postpone Action	Postpone Definitely	**"I move that the motion be postponed to . . ."**	Majority
Limit Debate	Limit Debate	**"I move that the debate on this motion be limited to (one) speech of (two) minutes for each member."**	Two-thirds
End Debate	Previous Question	**"I move the previous question."**	Two-thirds

TWO COMMONLY MISUSED MOTIONS

Postpone Indefinitely and Lay on the Table

The careful reader or student of Robert will have noticed that the lowest-ranked subsidiary motion, **postpone indefinitely**, and the highest-ranked subsidiary motion, **lay on the table**, have been omitted from Chart 1.

The author has omitted these motions deliberately. This book is designed as a practical and elementary guide to the commonly used and essential motions. The rarely used postpone indefinitely and usually misused lay on the table were considered unsuitable for this work.

Briefly, postpone indefinitely, the lowest-ranked subsidiary motion, is a motion to *kill* a main motion. It avoids a direct vote on the question on the floor. I call it the "straw vote" motion. It can be used to test the strength of a motion that a faction opposes. It was designed as a courtesy motion, to prevent a direct vote on a question that might be embarrassing to the group.

Example

Mr. C, the secretary of the Green Acres Association, has announced that he is running for the state senate. Mrs. G, a well-meaning member, makes the motion that the Green Acres Association support Mr. C in his bid for office.

The members are in the embarrassing position of perhaps voting against Mr. C, who has been a loyal and hardworking member of the association. Mr. R, a member well versed in parliamentary procedure, moves to postpone indefinitely the motion.

The group now does not have to risk voting against Mr. C, but rather the vote is on the motion to postpone indefinitely.

Lay on the table, the highest-ranked subsidiary motion, is generally misunderstood and misused by the public. The motion is frequently made that the group "table the motion" with the intent that the group clear the floor and "get rid of" the motion.

Lay on the table was also designed as a courtesy motion, allowing a group to set aside a question by a majority vote for something more important, such as the arrival of a speaker. Because this motion has the highest rank, it cannot be amended or debated.

Lay on the table is *out of order* when used to kill or avoid dealing with a measure. (*Robert's Rules of Order Newly Revised*, pages 208–209.)

Example

Back at the Green Acres Association, during discussion of the proposal to construct a playground, a member rises and says, **"I move to table the motion."**

The presiding officer should ask, **"Is it your intent to kill or dispose of the motion regarding the playground?"** If the answer is, "YES," the presiding officer states, **"That motion is out of order."**

Had the member moved to **"Table the motion until the next meeting,"** the presiding officer would have realized that the member's intent was to use the motion to postpone and would have handled it accordingly.

9

Privileged Motions

Privileged motions are not related to the business on the floor, but to the rights of members and the organization. They are of such importance that they have the right to interrupt business. Because of their high privilege, they are *undebatable.*

Privileged motions have rank among themselves and take precedence over all other motions.

Order of Rank from Lowest to Highest

Questions of Privilege
Recess
Adjourn

QUESTIONS OF PRIVILEGE

Questions of privilege relate to the rights of the organization or any of its members. The motion enables a member to interrupt business on the floor to state an urgent request. It is in order only when the comfort, dignity, safety, or reputation of the organization or any individual member is at stake.

There are two forms of privilege. One, known as **general privilege**, affects the organization and its meeting; the other, known as **personal privilege**, affects individual members.

Examples

GENERAL PRIVILEGE

"We cannot hear the speaker."

"The members in the back of the room did not receive the printed resolution."

PERSONAL PRIVILEGE

"The speaker is misstating my remarks."

Parliamentary Rules of Privilege

- The Chair usually rules as to whether privilege is important enough to interrupt business. A member cannot claim privilege and make a speech! The Chair should rule such behavior out of order.
- If motions of privilege are made when no business is pending, they may be debated and amended.
- The speaker who was interrupted again has the floor when the question of privilege is settled.

RECESS

Recess proposes a short intermission in the meeting. It temporarily suspends business, which is resumed at the same point at the end of the intermission.

The motion should state the length of the recess or the time for reconvening. The purpose of the recess might be for lunch, counting ballots, or similar matters.

Example

"The time is 12:30 and I move that we recess for lunch."

Parliamentary Rules of Recess

- Recess must be seconded.
- It cannot be debated.
- It can be amended, but only as to the length or time of the recess.
- It requires a majority vote.

ADJOURN

To **adjourn** means to close the meeting. An adjournment can be made while business is pending *provided that* the rules of the group provide for another meeting. When business is pending and the motion to adjourn is adopted, the unfinished business is carried over to the next meeting.

Example

"I move that we adjourn as the hour is late."

Parliamentary Rules of Adjourn

- Adjourn must be seconded.
- It is out of order when a member has the floor.
- It cannot be debated.
- It cannot be amended.
- It requires a majority vote.

CHART 2 **WHAT DO I SAY?**
Privileged Motions from Lowest to Highest Rank

TO DO THIS	MOTION	YOU SAY THIS	VOTE REQUIRED
Take Care of Noise or Temperature	Question of Privilege	**"We cannot hear in the back of the room."**	Chair Rules
Take Intermission	Recess	**"I move that we recess for . . ."**	Majority
Close Meeting	Adjourn	**"I move that we adjourn."**	Majority

10

Incidental or Unranked Motions

Incidental motions relate to procedure and not directly to the question on the floor. They are "incidental" to the main motion, brought about by chance in the process of the meeting. When an incidental motion is made, it must be acted upon before business can continue.

Incidental motions have *no rank* among themselves and may be applied to any main motion. They are decided as they arise. Incidental motions are *usually undebatable* and can only *rarely be amended*.

POINT OF ORDER

Point of order is the motion to use if you feel the Chair is failing to operate within the rules. The effect of this motion alerts the membership to a breach of procedure as well as requiring the Chair to defend a ruling.

Example

MEMBER: **"I rise to a point of order."**

CHAIR: **"What is your point?"**

MEMBER: **"The amendment just made is out of order. The motion already has an amendment and an amendment to the amendment pending."**

CHAIR: **"Your point is well taken and the amendment is ruled out of order."**

APPEAL

Appeal is the motion that allows any two members to counter what they feel is an incorrect or unfair ruling of the Chair. This motion, if seconded, requires the Chair to submit the ruling to the vote of the group. The group may vote in favor of the ruling of the Chair or they may vote against the ruling, reversing it.

Example

MEMBER: **"I appeal the decision of the Chair, the amendment just offered is germane."**

CHAIR: **"An appeal has been made that the amendment just offered is germane. Shall the decision of the Chair stand as the judgment of the group?"** [Debate ensues.] **As many as are in favor of the decision of the Chair say aye. Those opposed, no."**

Note: The Chair puts the question in the affirmative, thus a majority vote sustains the ruling of the Chair.

Special Parliamentary Rules

- Appeal requires a second.
- It is debatable, but the debate has limits.
  A. No member is allowed to speak more than once, except the Chair, who speaks first in defense of the ruling and may again speak at the end, immediately before the vote.
- A majority vote in the negative is required to reverse the ruling of the Chair.

POINT OF INFORMATION

Point of information is the motion used to obtain additional information on the subject being considered.

Example

MEMBER: **"I rise to a point of information."**
CHAIR: **"What is your point?"**
MEMBER: **"What is the amount of the surplus in the maintenance fund and what financial impact will the construction of the playground have on the Green Acres Association?"**

PARLIAMENTARY INQUIRY

Parliamentary inquiry is a useful motion that enables the members to obtain parliamentary help.

Example

MEMBER: **"I rise to a parliamentary question."**
CHAIR: **"What is your question?"**
MEMBER: **"Is it in order to move that the question of constructing a playground be postponed to the next meeting?"**

DIVISION

Division allows *any one* member to demand that the Chair verify a vote. To verify a vote, the Chair must *retake* the vote in a manner in which the group can see and be assured of the correctness of the call. If division has been called on a voice vote, the Chair retakes the vote by asking for a rising vote or by a show of hands in a small group. If division is called on a rising vote, the Chair retakes the vote by asking for a *counted* rising vote. The member does not seek recognition, but sitting in his seat calls out, "Division."

Example

MEMBER: **"Division!"**
CHAIR: **"Division has been called. Those in favor will please rise. Those opposed will please rise. The nos have it and the motion is lost."**

DIVISION OF A QUESTION

Division of a question may be used when a motion or resolution contains several parts, and the group wishes to vote on each part separately.

Example

MEMBER: **"I move that the motion be divided and we vote on each part separately."**

CHAIR: **"The motion has been made that the question be divided. The separate parts of this motion are interdependent and the motion to divide is not in order."**

Parliamentary Requirements

- The parts of the motion must be able to stand alone for division of a question to be in order.
- It requires a second.
- It requires a majority vote.

OBJECTION TO THE CONSIDERATION OF A QUESTION

Objection to the consideration of a question is used when a member feels that it would be harmful for a particular motion to come before the group for discussion and vote. This motion is rarely used.

Example

MEMBER A: **"I move that the president be censured for his remarks to the press."**

MEMBER B: **"I object to the consideration of the question!"**

CHAIR: **"An objection has been raised to the consideration of the question. Shall the question be considered? As many as are in favor, raise your right hand. Those opposed will raise the**

right hand. There being two-thirds opposed, the question will not be considered."

Note: The motion is stated in the **affirmative**, so two-thirds of the members must vote in the **negative** to suppress the motion.

Parliamentary Requirements

- It does not require a second.
- It cannot be debated or amended.
- It requires a two-thirds vote.
- It must be made before debate has begun. Otherwise, consideration has already begun and it is too late to object.

PERMISSION TO WITHDRAW A MOTION

Permission to withdraw a motion allows a member who realizes he has made a hasty or ill-advised motion to withdraw it with the consent of the group. This device saves time in disposing of the motion. The presiding officer usually handles the request by use of general consent.

Example

MEMBER: **"Mr. President, I request that my motion be withdrawn."**

CHAIR: **"If there is no objection, the motion will be withdrawn.** [Pause.] **There being no objection, the motion is withdrawn."**

CHART 3 **WHAT DO I SAY?**

Incidental or Unranked Motions

(In order when they apply to business on the floor)

TO DO THIS	MOTION	YOU SAY THIS	VOTE REQUIRED
To Enforce Rules	Point of Order	**"I rise to a point of order."**	Chair Rules
Protest Ruling of Chairman	Appeal	**"I appeal the decision of the Chair."**	Majority
Request Information	Point of Information	**"I rise to a point of information."**	Given by Chair/ Authority
Request Parliamentary Help	Parliamentary Inquiry	**"I rise to a parliamentary question."**	Chair Rules
Demand a Verification of a Vote	Division	**Call out, "Division!"**	On Demand of One Member
To Separate Parts of a Motion	Division of a Question	**"I move that the motion be divided."**	Majority
To Remove an Improper Matter from the Floor	Object to Consideration	**"I object to the consideration of . . . "**	Two-thirds
To Withdraw a Motion I Made	Permission to Withdraw	**"I request that my motion be withdrawn."**	Majority

11

Restorative Motions or Motions That Bring a Question Back

Restorative motions allow a group to change its mind. They are a separate category because of their contradiction to the parliamentary rule that once a question has been decided it cannot be brought up again at the same meeting.

Robert says that *within limits,* members have the right to rethink a situation if they feel their decision has been made too quickly or without enough information.

The two most commonly used restorative motions are rescind and reconsider.

RESCIND

Rescind is the motion used to quash or nullify a previously adopted motion. It may strike out an entire motion, resolution, bylaw, and so on.

Special Parliamentary Rules

- Rescind is not in order when any action has already been taken as a result of the vote, such as any kind of contract when the other party has been notified.
- It must be seconded.
- It requires a two-thirds vote unless notice has been given at the previous meeting, either verbally or in writing. If notice has been given, the motion requires only a majority vote.

Example

MEMBER: **"I move to rescind the motion regarding construction of a playground due to the financial impact on the Green Acres Association."**

CHAIR: **"Our parliamentary authority, *Robert's Rules of Order,* states that the motion to rescind is not in order when action has been taken as a result of the original vote. As no contracts have been let for the playground, the motion is in order.**

"The motion to rescind requires a second, is open to debate, and requires a two-thirds vote for its adoption. Is there any discussion?" [Debate ensues.] **"The question is on rescinding the motion to construct a playground, as many as are in favor will please rise. Those opposed, please rise.**

"The motion to rescind is lost. The motion to construct a playground stands as the will of the group."

RECONSIDER

Reconsider is the motion that allows a group to reconsider the *vote* on a motion. It is a strictly American motion that can be useful. It enables a majority of the members, within a limited time, to bring back a motion for further consideration after it has been acted upon. Its purpose is to prevent hasty or ill-advised action.

Reconsider has special rules to prevent its *abuse* by a disgruntled minority, since it allows a question already decided to be brought up again.

Special Parliamentary Rules

- Rules limit who can make the motion. It can only be made by someone who voted on the prevailing (winning) side.
- It has a time limit. It must be made on the same day that the vote to be reconsidered was taken. In a convention, it may be made on the next succeeding calendar day, but no later.
- It requires a second.
- It may be debated and it opens up the motion to which it is applied to debate.
- It requires only a majority vote.
- It may be made and seconded while other business is pending because of its time limit. However, it is not debated and voted on until the business on the floor is completed.
- All action that might come out of the original motion is stopped at the time that reconsider is

made and seconded. This is the main value of the motion, and it should be made as quickly as the situation calling for it is recognized.

Example

CHAIR: **"The motion has been made to reconsider the vote on asking Creative Playgrounds to present a proposal with cost estimates for the construction of a playground.**

"Our parliamentary authority states that the motion is only in order if made on the same day the original vote was taken or the next succeeding calendar day in convention. Therefore, the time limit of the motion has been met.

***"Robert's Rules* further states that the motion must be made by one who voted on the prevailing or winning side. How did you vote?"**

MEMBER: **"I voted for hiring Creative Playgrounds."**

CHAIR: **"The motion is in order. Is there a second?** [The motion is seconded.] **The motion has been made and seconded to reconsider the vote on asking Creative Playgrounds to present a proposal and cost estimates for the playground. Is there any discussion?"**

(Perhaps it has come to light that Creative Playgrounds has just filed for bankruptcy.)

CHAIR: **"As many are in favor of reconsidering the vote on asking Creative Playgrounds to present a proposal say aye. Those opposed say no. The ayes have it and the motion now on the floor is that Creative Playgrounds be asked to present a**

proposal for construction of a playground with cost estimates."

The original motion is now back on the floor. It may be amended, committed, or postponed before it is again put to a vote.

CHART 4 **WHAT DO I SAY?**
Restorative Motions or Motions That Bring a Question Back

TO DO THIS	MOTION	YOU SAY THIS	VOTE REQUIRED
To Change a Decision	Rescind	**"I move to rescind the motion to . . ."**	Two-thirds
To Bring Back a Motion for Revote	Reconsider*	**"I move to reconsider the vote on . . ."**	Majority

*Special Rules apply to this motion.

1. It must be made by someone who voted on the winning side.
2. It must be made *same day* or *next day* in a convention.

12

Resolutions

A **resolution** is nothing more than a main motion submitted in writing. Resolutions are generally used when an organization wishes to publish policy, principles, and sentiments or when more formality is desired.

There are two parts to a resolution. The first part is known as the **preamble** and begins with "Whereas." The preamble should be limited to providing the reasons for the resolution and any background information that might strengthen it. The second part of the resolution begins with "RESOLVED" and contains the motion to be adopted.

A brief, well-written resolution is more effective than a long, windy one. A preamble is not a parliamentary requirement, and should not be used merely for the sake of form.

EXAMPLE

Whereas,	The use of parliamentary procedure safeguards the democratic process; and
Whereas,	Parliamentary procedure is complex; therefore, be it
RESOLVED,	That the Green Acres Association purchase copies of *Robert's Rules in Plain English, Second Edition* for all of the officers.

The punctuation of a properly written resolution is important to note. Each clause is written as a separate paragraph punctuated with a semicolon. The only period appears at the end, no matter how lengthy the resolution. The beginning word of each clause in the preamble and "That" in the resolved section are capitalized. Please review the example.

ACTING ON A RESOLUTION

The **resolves** of a resolution are stated by the presiding officer and acted upon first. They are handled like any other main motion and are open to amendment. Once the resolves are adopted, the preamble is presented. The reason for presenting the preamble last is that any amendment of the resolves may require amendment of the preamble.

Example

"The resolution, resolved, that the Green Acres Association purchase copies of *Robert's Rules in Plain English, Second Edition,* for all of the officers is on the floor. Is there any discussion?"

Mr. P rises. "I move to amend the resolution by striking out the words 'for all of the officers' and inserting 'for the president.'"

The president states the amendment and takes the vote. The Green Acres Association, being wise, defeated the amendment. The resolution was adopted.

13

Voting

A **vote** is the means by which an individual member expresses a choice in a group. The result of the vote determines the action a group will take.

TYPES OF VOTES

- A **majority vote** is more than half of the votes cast.
  - A. The basic requirement for approval of an action or a choice except when a rule provides for a higher vote to adopt.

Example

Thirty votes have been cast. Sixteen votes are in favor, fourteen votes are opposed. The motion is adopted.

- A two-thirds vote has at least twice as many votes on the winning side as on the losing side. A vote of one-third plus one can defeat a proposition.

Example

Thirty votes have been cast. Twenty-one votes are in favor, nine votes are opposed. The motion is adopted.

A quick way to determine whether a motion requiring a two-thirds vote has carried is to multiply the negative vote by two. This number *must* be equal to or less than the number of the affirmative votes for the question to carry. ($2 \times 9 = 18$; 21 is greater than 18 and the motion is adopted.)

- A **plurality vote** is the largest number of votes given any candidate or proposition when there are three or more choices.

Example

Thirty votes have been cast for three candidates. Mr. A receives thirteen votes, Mr. B has twelve, and Mr. C gets five. Mr. A is elected even though he did not receive a majority.

A plurality vote never decides an election *unless* the bylaws specify that "a plurality shall elect."

METHODS OF VOTING

Voice Vote

Voting by voice is the usual method of voting when the motion *does not* require more than a majority.

The Chair calls for the affirmative first. **"All those in favor, please say aye."**

The negative vote is next called for. **"All those opposed, say no."** The negative vote *must always* be taken even though the Chair feels the affirmative vote has been sufficient to pass the motion.

The Chair makes the decision regarding the vote *by what he hears*. A voice vote may be difficult to judge. If the results are uncertain, it is important to *verify* the vote by taking a second vote with a *rising vote* or in a small group by a *show of hands*.

Example

"The Chair is in doubt. As many are in favor will please rise. Thank you. Those opposed will please rise. Thank you."

Rising Vote or Show of Hands

A rising vote or show of hands should be taken for *all* motions requiring a *two-thirds vote*. A voice vote cannot accurately determine a two-thirds vote.

If a motion requires a two-thirds vote, the Chair should inform the group of that.

Example

"This motion requires a two-thirds vote to adopt, which is a rising vote. All in favor will please rise. Thank you. All opposed will please rise. Thank you."

Verifying a Rising Vote

A **counted rising vote** is the clearest way for the Chair to determine an inconclusive rising vote. Any member may move that the vote be counted. This motion requires a second and a majority to adopt.

Example

The Chair announces that a counted rising vote will be taken. Instructions are given. **"Members in favor will please rise, count off, and be seated immediately after counting. The count will begin at the members' far left of each aisle and move to the right. Will Mr. L and Mr. M please serve as floor tellers to assist with the count."**

This method allows the group to see and hear the vote and to be convinced of the accuracy.

Ballot Vote

Each voter writes his choice on a piece of paper when voting is by ballot. It is primarily used to protect the voters' right to secrecy.

Ballot voting is used only if specified in the bylaws or ordered by the group. A vote by ballot can be *ordered* by a majority vote and may be the best means of voting when the issue is a divisive one.

The ballot may be an official printed form or merely a slip of paper. It can contain more than one question, and voters indicate their choices by making an "X" in the appropriate box or by writing "YES" or "NO."

Directions for marking the ballot must be absolutely clear.

The Chair appoints "tellers" to distribute, collect, and count the ballots. The tellers then report the results to the Chair, who announces the result of the vote.

Example

"The Chair appoints Mr. L and Mr. M to serve as tellers. The tellers will please distribute slips of paper. If you wish to vote for the proposition, please write 'yes' on the ballot. If you wish to vote against the proposition, please write 'no' on the ballot. [Pause while ballots are marked.] **The tellers will please collect and count the ballots, reporting the results to the Chair."**

A brief recess may be called while the tellers count. When the tellers have completed the count, they report the results to the presiding officer. The Chair announces the vote.

"There are 152 votes in favor and 98 votes opposed. The motion to construct a playground has been adopted."

In all methods of voting, **abstentions** are *not* counted. Only the number of votes cast is counted in determining a majority or two-thirds vote unless a special rule is stated in the bylaws.

General Consent

General consent is an informal agreement of the group, the method by which action is taken without a formal vote or on occasion without a motion. The Chair initiates the procedure. General consent is a valuable technique in expediting business. It quickly disposes of matters of routine business or those matters on which the Chair senses the group is in agreement. The approval and correction of minutes is an example of business that is usually handled by general consent.

Examples

- **"Are there any corrections to the minutes?** [Pause.] **There being none, the minutes are approved as read."**
- **"If there is no objection, we will take a ten-minute recess while the ballots are being counted.** [Pause.] **There being no objection, the meeting is recessed for ten minutes."**

The presiding officer always pauses after asking if there is any objection. If there is *any* objection, the matter is put to a vote in the usual way.

A member may object because he feels it is important to have a formal vote and dispel any suspicion of railroading.

A Tie Vote

A **tie vote** is a lost vote because a majority was not obtained. *The Chair is not compelled to break a tie!* While the Chair has a right to vote as a member, I recommend that he not vote unless the vote is by ballot. The Chair should appear impartial.

When a tie occurs, half of the group is opposed to the motion. If the issue is a divisive one, perhaps it is best for it to be defeated. Time heals, and the same question may always be reintroduced at a future meeting. In fact, it may occasionally be wise for the Chair to cast a vote in a majority of one to *create a tie*.

A Proxy Vote

A **proxy vote** is a written power of attorney given to one person to cast a vote on another's behalf. In most organizations, membership is individual, personal, and not transferrable, so proxy voting is not allowed.

Example

Mr. A is to be out of town at the time of the next meeting of the Green Acres Association, when the vote on the construction of the playground will occur. He writes out permission for Mr. B to cast his vote against the project. The president rules that Mr. B may not vote for Mr. A because proxies are not allowed.

It is a parliamentary principle that warm bodies must be *present* to vote in ordinary societies.

A Mail Vote

A printed ballot and return envelope are mailed to each member. The bylaws *must* state that a mail vote is permitted. It may be used when a vote of the full membership is desired, such as the election of officers or amendments to the bylaws.

Example

The bylaws of the Green Acres Association state that the election of officers shall be by mail vote. The association prints ballots and mails them and a return envelope to each member.

Electronic Voting

Electronic voting utilizes a system whereby each member votes by use of an individual keypad. This is the same as a **roll call** vote. It is only used by large organizations with the means to acquire an electronic system.

IV

The Organization

14

Bylaws

Robert defines **bylaws** as a document adopted by an organization that contains the basic rules for governing itself. Bylaws define the primary objectives of an organization and describe how that organization will function.

Bylaws should *help,* not *hinder,* an organization. They should serve to strengthen and protect a group, ensuring fulfillment of the purposes for which it was organized.

Good bylaws are concise, clear in meaning and well organized so that they are easy to use. They should never be unduly restrictive.

Bylaws must be consistent with the current practices and legal requirements of the state in which the organization is chartered.

Each sentence should be complete so that it cannot be quoted out of context. Any exceptions to or qualifications of a rule should be included *within the sentence to which they apply*. The words commonly used for exceptions are "except that" or "provided that."

Good bylaws give a clear picture of the way in which individual members relate to the structure of the organization.

CORPORATE CHARTER

The **corporate charter** is a legal instrument that sets forth the name and object of the organization and any other information that may be required by state or federal law.

Incorporation is necessary if the organization is to own property, make legally binding contracts, or inherit legacies.

A corporate charter should be drafted by an attorney and processed in accordance with the legal requirements of the state in which the organization is chartered.

The corporate charter *supersedes* all other rules of an organization and should be printed preceding the bylaws. Nothing in the charter can be suspended by the organization itself, so it should contain only the information absolutely necessary to obtain it.

STANDING RULES

Standing rules are those rules that relate to the details of administration. They may be adopted without previous notice and by a majority vote.

They may be rescinded and amended without notice.

AFFILIATED ORGANIZATIONS

Organizations that are affiliated with a parent organization, either state or national, must concur with the requirements of the bylaws of the parent organization. The local unit should not adopt provisions from the parent organization's bylaws that have no local application in a desire to conform.

SUGGESTED FORM FOR BYLAWS

Article I: Name

Article II: Object (Purpose)
A general statement as this article sets the boundaries within which the organization can function.

Article III: Members

Section 1. Classes of Membership (such as active, associate, honorary, etc.)

Section 2. Eligibility or Qualifications for Membership (including methods for granting membership)

Section 3. Fees or Dues

Section 4. Rights of Membership (optional unless a labor organization)

Section 5. Resignations and Disciplinary Action

Article IV: Officers

Section 1. List in Order of Rank (such as president, vice president, etc.)

Section 2. Duties

Section 3. Term of Office

Section 4. Nominations and Elections

Article V: Meetings

Section 1. Regular Meetings

Section 2. Annual Meeting

Section 3. Special Meetings

Section 4. Quorum

Article VI: Board of Directors

Section 1. Composition

Section 2. Powers

Section 3. Meetings

Section 4. Quorum

Article VII: Executive Committee

This article is usual in an organization that has a large board or one in which the board members have to travel long distances to attend meetings. An **executive committee** is composed of a specified number of board members who have the power of the board of directors between meetings of the board. It is a board within a board.

Article VIII: Committees

Each standing committee should be listed in a separate section containing:

- the name of the committee;
- the number of members;
- the manner of selection; and
- duties.

The last section of this article is "Special Committees," which permits the establishment "of such special committees as necessary to carry on the work of the organization."

Article IX: Parliamentary Authority

Article X: Amendment of the Bylaws

Prescribes the procedure, usually requiring previous notice and a two-thirds vote.

Article XI: Dissolution (required by the IRS for all tax-exempt organizations)

A **dissolution clause** states what will happen to the assets should the organization be dissolved.

If the organization is incorporated, the dissolution clause may be contained in the articles of incorporation and does not need to be restated.

CHANGING BYLAWS

- The bylaws of an organization should be reviewed from time to time to ensure that they reflect the current needs and practices of the group.
- Bylaws may be changed by either **amendment** or **revision**. The distinction between the two is important.
    A. Amendment opens only specific sections to change for which notice has been given.
    B. Revision opens the entire document to review and change. It involves rewriting the existing document and substituting a newly written document.
- Bylaws usually require *previous notice* and a *two-thirds vote* for change. When drafting the published notice, it is important to be specific as to whether notice is being given for amendments or a revision. Do you want to open up several articles for amendment or the whole document?
- The proposed amendments are placed on the agenda under General Orders just before New Business.
- When three or more alternatives for an amendment are presented, the *least inclusive* amendment is presented first and the *most inclusive* amendment last.

Example

Three different amendments have been proposed to increase the dues of the Green Acres Association.

The dues are presently $100 per year. The increases proposed are to $150, $200, and $250 per year. Being the smallest increase, $150 is put to a vote first. If this amendment receives a two-thirds vote, it is adopted and the other amendments are not presented. Should the increase to $150 be lost, the increase to $200 would next be put to a vote.

- Proposed amendments to bylaws may be amended by a majority vote at the meeting at which they are presented. A motion to amend the proposed amendment may not exceed the scope of the notice.

Example

The proposed amendment to increase the dues from $100 to $250 per year is on the floor. It would be in order to offer an amendment for a sum *less* than $250 but not in order to offer an amendment for *more* than $250. An amendment to **"strike out $250 and insert $225"** is in order. An amendment to **"strike out $250 and insert $300"** is not in order. It exceeds the scope of the notice given.

- Many organizations are beginning to operate in a leaner fashion with fewer officers and smaller boards. Elected officers should not be "amended" out of office before the expiration of their terms. The organization essentially has a contract with officers *already elected* and any action taken to terminate the contract should be done with consideration. A timetable for the abolition of the offices should be developed. This timetable should not be incorporated into the printed bylaws.

- A **proviso** should be attached that details the timetable for the phasing out of the positions. Such provisions are numbered and attached to the draft of the bylaws on a separate sheet headed "Proviso Relating to Transition." This prevents cluttering up the new bylaws with the details of the transition period.

Example

The Bylaw Chairman states, **"I move the adoption of the following amendments with the attached provisos."**

- Unless the vote is almost unanimous, close votes on the adoption of bylaw amendments or revision should be counted and recorded in the minutes.

Amendments to Amendments of Bylaws

- Amendments to bylaws are main motions and may therefore have primary and secondary amendments to them.
- Amendments to amendments are *limited in the extent of change* for which notice was given. Amendments *may not* exceed the scope of the notice. This prevents a minority from proposing

a slight amendment to a bylaw and then taking advantage of the absent members by proposing a greater change.

- Amendments to amendments *may not* introduce any new changes not specified in the notice.

Example

An amendment has been proposed to increase the annual dues of the Green Acres Association. That same article also contains the deadline for the payment of dues. An amendment changing the fiscal year or deadline for payment is out of order.

- Amendments to amendments are adopted by a majority vote. However, the amended amendment still requires a two-thirds vote.

HANDLING BYLAW AMENDMENTS

- Bylaw amendments become effective *immediately* upon adoption and cannot be reconsidered. If the amendments are not to go into effect immediately, the motion to adopt should contain a *proviso*.

Example

"Upon direction of the Bylaws Committee, I move the adoption of the proposed amendments with the proviso that they shall not go into effect until the close of the annual meeting."

- It is recommended that a revision or a series of amendments be presented **by paragraphs (seriatim)** to save time in the voting process. This method opens each proposed amendment to debate and amendment separately and in order. One vote is taken at the conclusion when all of the proposed amendments have been presented. All of the proposed amendments are adopted or defeated by a standing two-thirds vote.

Script for a Presiding Officer

CHAIR: **"The next business in order is the proposed revision of the bylaws. If there is no objection, the revision will be considered by paragraphs.** [Chair explains procedure.] **Each article will be considered and discussed separately, at which time it may be amended. One vote will be taken at the end.** [Pause to see if anyone objects.] **There being no objection, the amendments will be considered by paragraphs. The bylaws chairman will please proceed."**

BYLAWS CHAIR: **"Mister President** [Chairman, Speaker, etc.], **by direction of the Bylaws Committee, I move the adoption of the following revision of the bylaws."**

CHAIR: **"It has been moved that the following revision be adopted."** (A second

	is not required as the motion comes from a committee.)
BYLAWS CHAIR:	**"Article I . . ."** (The chairman explains the change and the rationale for it.)
CHAIR:	**"Is there any discussion of the proposed article ____, section ____?"**

Amendments are adopted by a majority vote. This procedure continues until all of the articles in the proposed revision have been presented.

Conclusion

CHAIR:	**"The question is on the adoption of the proposed revision of the bylaws. Are you ready for the question?** [Pauses.] **All in favor of the adoption of the proposed revision will please rise. Those opposed will please rise. Thank you. There being two-thirds in favor of the revision, the revision is adopted."**

GIVING NOTICE OF BYLAW AMENDMENTS

The general membership may not be familiar with the bylaws. It is important that the written notice be crystal clear as to the changes suggested and the reasons for the changes. If the membership is educated and informed, valuable time is saved during the discussion of the amendments.

I recommend that notice be given with a three-column form to clearly indicate the proposed amendments, how the amended section will read, and the reasons for the proposed change.

A Sample Form for Proposed Amendments

The words enclosed in parenthesis and underlined (____) are to be deleted. The words in **bold** are to be added.

PROPOSED AMENDMENTS	IF ADOPTED, WILL READ	RATIONALE
Article III, Section 3. Dues		
The annual dues shall be (<u>$150.00</u>) **$200** payable on or before December 1.	The annual dues shall be $200 payable on or before December 1.	The increase is needed to maintain a balance in the maintenance fund.

15

The Board of Directors

The board is a permanent part of the organization provided for in the bylaws. Members of the board are temporary agents elected to act in an administrative capacity.

- The board has only the *power delegated* to it in the bylaws or by vote of the general membership.
- The board operates under the bylaws, the parliamentary authority, and any state or federal laws applying to it.
- The board *cannot* delegate its power/responsibilities to others. The board may appoint committees to work under its supervision. These committees of the board report directly to the board and the responsibility for any decisions rests directly with the board.
- The board *cannot rescind* or be in conflict with any action taken by the general membership.

CONDUCT OF BUSINESS IN A BOARD MEETING

- Board meetings are confidential unless other provisions apply, such as the "Sunshine Law." Business is not discussed with other members of the organization until that information is issued to all members or to the public.
- Members may be invited to attend meetings to give information or expert advice, but do not necessarily remain for deliberations. They are never allowed to vote.
- The formality of meetings will depend on the size and custom of the group. Generally, parliamentary rules are more relaxed in a small board than in the meeting of a large board.
  The differences are:
  - board members may make motions and speak while seated;
  - motions do not require a second;
  - debate is not limited; and
  - the chairman may make motions, debate, and vote without leaving the chair.

  Parliamentary requirements are:
  - motions must be clearly stated by the Chair;
  - discussion is limited to the subject of the motion on the floor; and
  - only one person may speak at a time.
- It may be necessary to apply parliamentary rules as strictly as in a general membership meeting if controversy develops.

16

Parliamentary Requirements of Conventions

After the opening ceremonies of a convention, there are *three required procedures*:

1. The adoption of the report of the Credentials Committee
2. The adoption of the Convention Rules
3. The adoption of an Agenda/Program

CREDENTIALS COMMITTEE REPORT

The Credentials Committee determines the number of voting members present through registration, which may be conducted by the committee or by staff. The number of voting members registered determines whether a quorum is present. (A quorum is the minimum number of members that must be present to legally transact business. It is usually stated in the bylaws.)

- The **credentials report** must be given first even if delegates are still registering. An incomplete credentials report is called a **preliminary report**. The complete report is given at a later time when registration is complete.
- The credentials report must be adopted, either by a motion made by the chairman or by general consent.
- After the report is adopted, the presiding officer declares a quorum present and the meeting to be in official session.

Example

"A quorum being present, this convention is in official session."

In the case of a preliminary report, the usual case: **"The credentials chairman will give a complete report as soon as those figures are available."**

ADOPTION OF THE CONVENTION RULES

Special rules are usually necessary to limit the length and number of speeches allowed delegates, the length of reports, and so on due to the size of the meeting and the amount of business to be conducted.

- The chairman of the Rules Committee presents the rules and moves, **"The adoption of the convention rules as printed in the program."**
- No second is required, as this motion comes from a committee.

- A *two-thirds vote* (which is a rising vote) is required due to the limitation of the rights of members.
- The Chair declares that the rules are adopted. **"There being two-thirds in favor, the rules are adopted."**

ADOPTION OF THE AGENDA/PROGRAM

- The Chair may use general consent to adopt the program. **"If there is no objection, the program will be adopted as printed.** [Pause.] **There being no objection, the program is adopted."**

The delegates have the right to offer amendments at the time each of these motions is presented for action. The credentials report may be amended to seat additional delegates. The rules may be amended to be either more restrictive or more liberal. The program may be amended to change the order of business.

SPECIAL RULES FOR A CONVENTION OR ANNUAL MEETING

The purpose of adopting special rules is to expedite business and ensure the principle that each member has the privilege of the floor while protecting the right of the organization to accomplish its business.

Sample Rules

GENERAL PROCEDURES

1. Members and guests shall register and display identification badges before being admitted to the business session.
2. When seeking recognition and permission of the floor, the member shall proceed to the microphone in his area and give his name (and chapter).
3. Oral reports by committee chairmen shall not exceed five minutes.
4. No recordings shall be made of the proceedings other than those approved by the board of directors.

MOTIONS, RESOLUTIONS, AND ANNOUNCEMENTS

1. All motions shall be written, signed, and sent immediately to the desk of the recording secretary.
2. Only the **resolves** of a resolution shall be debated and acted upon.
3. Announcements shall be in writing, signed by the person under whose authority the announcement is issued, and sent to the recording secretary.

DEBATE AND VOTING

1. Debate shall be limited to two minutes for each speaker, who shall not speak more than twice on the same question. No member shall

speak more than once to the same question unless everyone who wishes has spoken.

A SUGGESTED CONVENTION AGENDA

Registration (list hours)

Opening Ceremonies:
A. Welcoming Remarks
B. Invocation
C. Pledge of Allegiance to the Flag of the United States
D. Roll Call (usually only in elected assemblies)

Introductions

Credentials Report

Convention Rules

Convention Program

Elections

Reports of Officers

Report of Auditor

Report of Executive Board

Reports of Standing Committees

Reports of Special Committees

Special Orders

Unfinished Business and General Orders

New Business

Announcements, Program

Adjournment Sine Die

("Sine Die" means "without day," or never to meet again as each convention will have a different membership with the election of different delegates.)

V

Electronic Meetings

17

An Introduction to Electronic Parliamentary Procedures

As the cost and difficulty of travel has escalated in recent years, organizations of all kinds are looking for cost-effective ways to share information and reach decisions by electronic means. Government agencies, large businesses, and educational institutions have led the way in electronic communication. However, as technology has become more accessible, more affordable, and easier to use, more organizations, especially those with national or multinational boards, are beginning to hold electronic meetings.

The material in the following chapters is not found in *Robert's Rules of Order Newly Revised*. It is the author's guide to how technological innovations can be used by organizations without jeopardizing the parliamentary principles of democratic organizations.

DEFINITIONS

An electronic meeting is a meeting held in two or more places with the participants using electronic means of communication. **Teleconferencing** is a general term for any interactive communication between three or more people using telecommunications links at two or more places. There are many types of teleconferencing, including videoconferencing, computer conferencing, and audio conferencing.

- Videoconferencing is like a live TV program that uses satellites to specifically licensed sites, allowing spoken and visual communication among participants around the world. Until the mid-1990s, hardware costs made videoconferencing prohibitively expensive for most organizations, but that situation is changing. According to Webopedia, many analysts believe that videoconferencing will be one of the fastest-growing segments of the computer industry in the latter half of this decade.
- Computer conferencing uses printed communication through computer terminals.
- Audio conferencing (conference calls) uses telephone lines to link participants in spoken communication in multiple locations.

ADVANTAGES OF ELECTRONIC MEETINGS

Some advantages of electronic meetings are:

- Electronic meetings reduce the costs of large national and international meetings.

- They are good for simple problem solving, information sharing, and procedural tasks.
- They increase attendance among members who are unable to attend due to time constrictions, climate, or transportation problems.
- Group members often participate more fully in a well-moderated teleconference than in a face-to-face meeting.

DISADVANTAGES OF ELECTRONIC MEETINGS

- Technical and equipment failures may occur.
- Electronic meetings are more impersonal, making it difficult to create an atmosphere of easy rapport.
- Difficulties may be encountered in deciding complex issues that require negotiation.
- Members may lack familiarity with the skills required to conduct such meetings.
- Greater member preparation is necessary for a productive meeting.
- Electronic meetings present difficulties in assigning the floor (determining the speaking order) of members.

DANGERS OF ELECTRONIC MEETINGS

It is essential to protect the democratic principles that sustain our decision making in groups of all kinds. While teleconferencing facilitates linking people, it does not change the complexity of the problems of group communication and decision making, and can even exacerbate them. While taking advantage of all that technology has to offer, members must gauge for themselves whether teleconferencing will hinder or help their organization. It is important not to underestimate the merits of interaction in face-to-face meetings. It has been said that "virtual" meetings will replace "real" meetings when "virtual" honeymoons replace "real" ones.

PARLIAMENTARY REQUIREMENTS

Parliamentary law dictates that decisions be made by a majority of members present at a duly-called meeting at which a quorum is present. The parliamentary requirements for electronic meetings are as follows:

- The bylaws must *state* that electronic meetings may be held.
- Proper notice of the meeting must be given.
- A quorum must be present.
- Each member must be given an opportunity to express his views and to listen to the views of others.
- A legal vote must be obtained by written ratification to verify the vote of an electronic meeting.

SPECIAL RULES REQUIRED

Special rules need to be developed to ensure that the democratic process is preserved, such as:

- a means of verifying members and a quorum (e.g., the chairman calls the name of all the members);
- rules regarding debate (e.g., **"No one may speak more than once until all have had an opportunity to speak");**
- how a member obtains the floor (e.g., the member says, **"Mister Chairman,"** stating his name, and waits for the chairman to acknowledge him);
- how the vote is to be taken and verified (e.g., the chairman calls each member's name and asks that they vote yea or nay; obviously, a secret ballot is impossible); and
- **criteria** for when and how electronic meetings may be used.

IS YOUR GROUP READY?

If your board or association is beginning to ask about electronic meetings, the following questions should be considered:

- How comfortable are *all* the members with the idea of electronic meetings?
- Are all the members computer literate and do they all have e-mail addresses?
- Is an electronic meeting the most appropriate for the issue?
- Would the question require considerable discussion in a face-to-face meeting?

HOW TO BEGIN

Start using electronic meetings in information sharing and on less important, routine matters that you expect will require little or no discussion. If this is successful, then you may work in more substantive issues.

18

Videoconferencing

Videoconferencing is like a live TV show. Members can see each other on a computer screen and hear each other through their computer speakers. The images of participants can be either a permanent presence or voice activated. Permanent presence displays images of all the participants all the time. It may not be possible to see everyone clearly, but it may be helpful to see their reactions. Voice-activated models display only the face of the person speaking. The picture is clearer, but the reactions of the group members are missing.

HOW TO ORGANIZE A VIDEOCONFERENCE

- Develop rules for the conduct of the meeting.
- Prepare and distribute a detailed agenda. Attach any helpful reports or background information.
- Establish the time of the meeting. (This may be

difficult, as you may be working with multiple time zones.)

- Prepare a list of contact numbers in the event the connections fail to work.
- Develop a "minutes form" to record action agreed upon.
- Develop a "ratification form" that is sent to each member to sign and record his vote. This form is returned to the chairman.

DURING THE MEETING

- Open the meeting with a roll call and determine that all can hear and see you. Ask each member to introduce himself; this informs you that they can be seen and heard.
- Review the planned agenda.
- Review the *rules* of the meeting, especially as to how members obtain recognition and the floor.
- Leave longer pauses when recognizing members due to the time lag in transmission.
- Address members by name.
- *Clearly* state the question when it is time to open discussion.
- *Verify* votes by calling each member's name.
- Clearly *adjourn* the meeting.

VIDEOCONFERENCING ETIQUETTE

- Speak clearly and more slowly than normal.
- Keep body movements to a minimum.

- Dress in muted colors, avoiding loud plaids and stripes.
- Use the *mute* button when shuffling papers, coughing, and so on.

PARLIAMENTARY REQUIREMENTS FOR VIDEOCONFERENCING

- The bylaws must contain a statement permitting videoconferencing. This is usually in the "Meetings" section.

Example

Meetings of the directors or committees may be held by videoconferencing provided that all members participating can see and hear each other simultaneously.

- The bylaws should also state that signatures transmitted by facsimile transmission shall be deemed as valid.

19

The Conference Call (Audio Conferencing)

All states recognize that a duly-called meeting for a conference call at which a quorum is present is a valid meeting. A conference call allows all members to hear one another and fully participate in all business to be conducted.

HOW TO ORGANIZE AND RUN A CONFERENCE CALL

Before the Call

- Develop rules for the conduct of the meeting.
- Develop a conference call checklist (are all the telephone numbers current?).
- Develop a detailed meeting agenda form that should be sent to all members ahead of time (what business is to be considered and the order in which it will be considered).

- Develop a meeting minutes form to accurately record action agreed upon.
- Develop a "feedback form" that can be e-mailed to the participants. This allows members to review their impression of the meeting.
- Develop a "ratification form" that members sign and return by facsimile transmission or regular mail.

During the Call

- Open the meeting with a roll call (call all the names of the participants and have them answer so you know that all are connected).
- Review the rules, such as:
    1. Members shall identify themselves and request permission of the chairman before speaking.
    2. No member may speak more than two minutes at a time.
    3. No member may speak more than once until all who wish have spoken.
        - Introduce any new members so that all of the members know each other.
        - *Clearly* state the question when it is time to open discussion.
        - *Track* who is talking and call on those members who have not spoken.
        - *Verify* the vote by calling each member's name and asking how he wishes to vote.
        - End the call clearly, making certain that all members know that the meeting is adjourned.

CONFERENCE CALL ETIQUETTE

- Be on time.
- Take the call in a quiet location.
- Use a hardwired phone if possible (cellular phones and speaker phones tend to pick up ambient noise).
- Turn off your call-waiting.
- State your name before you begin talking as required by the rules.
- Respect the time limits set for debate.
- Do not put the phone on hold to perform another task.

VALIDATING ACTION

- Each member signs a written consent for action taken during the conference call (ratification).
- The action may be ratified at the next face-to-face meeting.

PARLIAMENTARY REQUIREMENTS

- The bylaws must contain a statement permitting teleconferencing (usually located in the "Meetings" section).

Example

Meetings of the directors or committees may be held by teleconferencing, provided that all the members participating can hear and speak to each other simultaneously.

- The bylaws should also state that signatures transmitted by facsimile transmission shall be deemed as valid.

A CAUTION REGARDING TELEPHONE POLLING

It should be emphasized that calling members of a board or committee and polling them regarding action to be taken does not meet the requirements for a meeting in any state. The important element of group deliberation is missing. Each member should be making a decision based on the exchange of ideas that occur in a regular meeting.

20

E-mail

E-mail is convenient, efficient, and economical. It is the most widely used and productive tool of Internet service. Tens of millions of messages fly across the wires every day.

USES IN ORGANIZATIONS

Meetings

Virtually every state has ruled that e-mail meetings are not valid meetings due to the legal principle that boards are authorized to deliberate and act as a group, not as individual members. *Robert's Rules of Order* states that *simultaneous* communication is essential to the deliberative nature of meetings.

Several parliamentarians have attempted to devise rules for e-mail meetings. The rules are extremely cumbersome and require extensive training to implement. A single motion might require as much as a week from its posting to action, and then it would not be considered legally valid.

Robert's Rules in Plain English, Second Edition **recommends against the attempted use of e-mail for meeting purposes.**

Uses

E-mail is extremely useful for the rapid dissemination of information and the economic use of office staff and supplies. The best parliamentary use of e-mail is to facilitate board meetings. Notices of meetings, minutes, and background information may be sent by e-mail provided all the members have e-mail addresses. Regular mail must be used for those members without e-mail.

Secrecy is not guaranteed in e-mail, so *no minutes of an executive session, personnel matters, or other sensitive material* may be sent by e-mail.

E-mail Policy

Any organization with an e-mail address should adopt an e-mail policy that clearly outlines the use of office e-mail, emphasizing that e-mail is a communication of the organization and is not for personal use. Any person with access to e-mail equipment has the ability to send any message anywhere at any time.

WHAT ABOUT CHAT ROOMS?

Chat rooms are a form of instant messaging that allow people to get together in cyberspace, reaching across continents to discuss common interests. Chat rooms differ from e-mail in that the typed messages are transmitted almost instantly and the other participants can type their responses immediately.

Chat rooms may be useful for small informational meetings (five to six people) in which each member has the technological know-how to participate. However, they should not be used for complex or sensitive issues that require an extensive amount of negotiation. Some means of verifying participants and developing a chat room model should be constructed before attempting to discuss the business of an organization. A legal vote cannot be determined in a chat room.

For all the above reasons, chat rooms should be used sparingly for informational purposes only. Technological advances now in the experimental stage will enhance the use of chat rooms. With the development of voice mail and the use of webcams and web phones, chat rooms will more nearly approximate videoconferencing.

AN EXAMPLE OF AN ELECTRONIC MEETING AT THE GREEN ACRES ASSOCIATION

It has come to the attention of the president of the Green Acres Association that the association swimming pool has suffered severe structural damage during the winter. If the pool is to be operational by the summer, repairs should be begun immediately.

Unfortunately, three of the five members of the executive committee are vacationing at their winter homes. The president is thus unable to obtain a quorum for a face-to-face meeting. He feels it is unwise to wait for their return to consider repairs. Consequently, the president turns to electronic means to solve the problem. He knows that all three have laptop computers with them, as he has received e-mails from each of them.

He decides on the following course of action. He obtains three estimates for the cost of the repair of the pool. He then e-mails the absent members:

- a detailed description of the problem;
- attaches a file of the three estimates obtained for the repair; and
- schedules a tentative date and time for a conference call, which he requests they confirm by e-mail.

All of the members, including absent ones, reply that they are available to take a conference call at the appointed date and time.

Being a capable chairman, Mr. A:

- checks all the telephone numbers to make certain of their accuracy;
- develops a detailed agenda;
- develops rules for the conduct of the meeting;
- develops a minutes meeting form; and
- develops a ratification form to be mailed to all members.

At the appointed time of the call, when connections have been made, he opens the meeting by calling each member's name so that he knows all are present and connected.

He opens the meeting by stating the problem with the swimming pool and reviewing the estimates obtained.

The members agree that the pool must be repaired in a timely fashion so that it can open on schedule for the summer season. Mr. C states that a friend of his felt that one of the bidders, Lazy Day Pools, had done shoddy work on his pool. The other two estimates are discussed, regarding the extent of repairs proposed and the cost. The members decide that Happy Pools should be awarded the job.

Mr. A then informs the group that a ratification form will be mailed to each member for their signatures to document the expenditure of such a large amount of money before he contacts Happy Pools. (Had facsimile machines been available to the three out-of-town members, the form could have been faxed to them and their completed forms faxed back.)

Thanks to electronic meetings, the Green Acres Association will hopefully have a fully operational pool by the beginning of swimming season.

CONCLUSION

As technology advances, becoming more accessible and economical, the feasibility of true electronic meetings will undoubtedly also increase. In considering the use of any new technology, the following must be taken into account:

- Does the technology meet the parliamentary requirements for a meeting?
- Does it meet the requirements of your state for a legally accepted meeting?

WEB SITES USED FOR REFERENCE

1. The National Association of Legal Services Developers at www.tcsg.org/nalsd.htm
2. The Pennsylvania State University at www.psu.edu
3. Teaching Support Services at www.tss.noguelnh.ca
4. The University of Warwick at www.Warwick.ac.uk
5. Washington Technology www.washingtontechnology.com
6. Webopedia at www.Webopedia.com

SUGGESTED READING AND STUDY

Robert's Rules in Plain English, Second Edition, is based on the standard parliamentary authority for most American organizations, *Robert's Rules of Order Newly Revised.*

The serious student of parliamentary procedure is encouraged to study that reference for additional and more detailed information than the material included in this book:

*Robert's Rules of Order Newly Revised,*10th ed. Cambridge, Mass: Perseus Publishing, 2000.

A GLOSSARY OF PARLIAMENTARY TERMS

abstain: To refrain from voting
acclamation: Unanimous consent
ad hoc committee: A special committee
adjourn: To end a meeting
adopt: To act in favor of a motion
agenda: A list of items to be taken up at a meeting
amend: To change a pending motion
amendment: A motion that changes a motion
appeal: A motion to object to a ruling of the chair
appoint: To assign to a committee or office
ballot vote: A secret vote, written on a piecc of paper
budget: A summary of anticipated income and expenses for the upcoming fiscal year
bylaws: The written rules for governing an organization
carried: To adopt a motion
Chair: The presiding officer
chat room: A form of instant messaging

circulated agenda: A prepared agenda which has been distributed to members prior to the meeting

commit: To send a motion to a small number of members for study

conference call: Telephone communication in which all participants can hear discussion simultaneously

debate: The formal discussion of a motion

debatable: A motion that is open to discussion

dilatory motion: An absurd or irrelevant motion

dilatory tactic: A misuse of parliamentary procedure

division: To call for a recount of the vote

electronic meetings: Meetings held in two or more places with telecommunication links

e-mail: Text messages sent from one person to another by means of a computer, a modem, and a telephone line

ex officio: A member of a committee because of the office held

executive committee: A small board within a board that has the power of the board between meetings

executive session: A secret session of members only

floor (as in "have the floor"): To be given permission to speak at a meeting

general consent: Unanimous approval of the group

germane: Closely related to and having a direct bearing upon

illegal ballot: A ballot that cannot be counted because it does not conform to the balloting rules

incidental motion: A motion that deals with questions of procedure

in order: Correct parliamentary procedure

legal vote: A vote cast by a member in good standing at a meeting where a quorum is present

limit debate: To reduce the number or length of speeches allowed

lost motion: A motion that has been defeated

main motion: A motion that introduces a subject to the group for discussion and action

majority vote: One more than half the votes cast

meeting: A gathering of members of an organization to conduct business

member: A person who has legally joined an organization

minority: Any number that is less than half the number of members present

minutes: The official written record of a meeting

motion: A proposal that some action be taken or an opinion expressed by the group

negative vote: A vote against the motion on the floor

new business: New matters brought for consideration

nomination: The formality of naming a person as a candidate for election to an office

ordered: Directed by vote of the organization

order of business: The schedule of business to be considered

out of order: Not correct from a parliamentary standpoint

parliamentary procedure: An established system of rules that govern the procedure in democratic meetings

pending: The question(s) that are under consideration

pending question: The last motion stated by the Chair

plurality vote: The largest number of votes when there are three or more choices

point of order: An objection made for improper procedure

preamble: The introduction to a resolution that begins with "whereas"

precedence: The rank or priority of consideration of a motion

prevailing side: The winning side

previous notice: A written notice before a meeting that a motion will be introduced

previous question: A motion to end debate and vote immediately

primary amendment: The first amendment to a motion

privileged motion: A motion related to the rights of members and the organization

pro tem: Temporary

proviso: A stipulation article that states a condition to the bylaws

proxy vote: A power of attorney given to one person to cast a vote on another's behalf

putting the question: Placing the motion before the group for a vote

question: A motion

question of privilege: A question that relates to the rights of the organization or its members

quorum: The number of members that must be present for the legal transaction of business

rank: The order in which one motion yields to another; see *precedence*

recess: To take a short intermission in a meeting

refer: To send the motion to a small group for consideration

renew: To bring a motion back at *another* meeting

report: A written or oral account of the work conducted by an officer or a committee

resolution: A formal written motion

resolves: The second part of a resolution that contains the motion for action

restorative motions: Motions that allow a main motion to be brought back to the floor

revision of bylaws: Rewriting the entire bylaw document

roll call vote: The name of each member is called and his vote is recorded

ruling: A decision made by the presiding officer

second: A second person agrees to have a motion considered

secondary amendment: An amendment to an amendment

secondary motion: Motion made while the main motion is still on the floor

seriatim: Consideration by paragraphs

session: A meeting or a series of connected meetings, as in a convention

standing rules: Rules that relate to the details of administration; they require only a majority vote to adopt, amend, or suspend

subsidiary motion: A class of motions that help to dispose of a main motion

teleconferencing: Communication between two or more people in two or more places

tellers: Members officially designated to count ballots or votes

tie vote: The same number of votes on each side

two-thirds vote: Two-thirds of the votes cast must be cast in the affirmative to adopt

unanimous vote: No dissenting vote

undebatable motion: A motion on which discussion is not allowed

unfinished business: Matters from a previous meeting postponed or brought over to the next meeting

voice vote: Members call out their vote by saying "aye" or "no"

vote: A formal decision, either positive or negative, made by members of a group in regard to a matter brought before it

yield: To give way when you have been assigned the floor

INDEX

CHARTS OF MOTIONS

CHART 1 **WHAT DO I SAY?**
Subsidiary Motions from Lowest to Highest Rank

TO DO THIS	**MOTION**	**YOU SAY THIS**	**VOTE REQUIRED**
Introduce Business	Main	**"I move that . . ."**	Majority
Change the Wording of a Motion	Amend	**"I move to amend the motion by . . ."** (adding words; striking out or substituting words)	Majority
Send to Committee	Commit	**"I move that the motion be referred to . . ."**	Majority
Postpone Action	Postpone Definitely	**"I move that the motion be postponed to . . ."**	Majority
Limit Debate	Limit Debate	**"I move that the debate on this motion be limited to (one) speech of (two) minutes for each member."**	Two-thirds
End Debate	Previous Question	**"I move the previous question."**	Two-thirds

CHART 2 **WHAT DO I SAY?**
Privileged Motions from Lowest to Highest Rank

TO DO THIS	**MOTION**	**YOU SAY THIS**	**VOTE REQUIRED**
Take Care of Noise or Temperature	Question of Privilege	**"We cannot hear in the back of the room."**	Chair Rules
Take Intermission	Recess	**"I move that we recess for . . ."**	Majority
Close Meeting	Adjourn	**"I move that we adjourn."**	Majority

CHART 3 **WHAT DO I SAY?**

Incidental or Unranked Motions

(In order when they apply to business on the floor)

TO DO THIS	**MOTION**	**YOU SAY THIS**	**VOTE REQUIRED**
To Enforce Rules	Point of Order	**"I rise to a point of order."**	Chair Rules
Protest Ruling of Chairman	Appeal	**"I appeal the decision of the Chair."**	Majority
Request Information	Point of Information	**"I rise to a point of information."**	Given by Chair/ Authority
Request Parliamentary Help	Parliamentary Inquiry	**"I rise to a parliamentary question."**	Chair Rules
Demand a Verification of the Vote	Division	**Call out, "Division!"**	On Demand of One Member
To Separate Parts of a Motion	Division of a Question	**"I move that the motion be divided."**	Majority
To Remove an Improper Matter from the Floor	Object to Consideration	**"I object to the consideration of . . . "**	Two-thirds
To Withdraw a Motion I Made	Permission to Withdraw	**"I request that my motion be withdrawn."**	Majority

CHART 4 **WHAT DO I SAY?**
Restorative Motions or
Motions That Bring a Question Back

TO DO THIS	MOTION	YOU SAY THIS	VOTE REQUIRED
To Change a Decision	Rescind	**"I move to rescind the motion to . . ."**	Two-thirds
To Bring Back a Motion for Revote	Reconsider*	**"I move to reconsider the vote on . . ."**	Majority

*Special Rules apply to this motion.

1. It must be made by someone who voted on the winning side.
2. It must be made *same day* or *next day* in a convention.

Medical Library
North Memorial Health Care
3300 Oakdale Avenue North
Robbinsdale, MN 55422